bricks

A GUIDE TO THE REPAIR OF HISTORIC BRICKWORK

Comhshaol, Oidhreacht agus Rialtas Áitiúil
Environment, Heritage and Local Government

DUBLIN
PUBLISHED BY THE STATIONERY OFFICE
To be purchased directly from:
Government Publications Sales Office
Sun Alliance House
Molesworth Street
Dublin 2

or by mail order from:
Government Publications
Postal Trade Section
Unit 20 Lakeside Retail Park
Claremorris
Co. Mayo

Tel: 01 – 6476834/37 or 1890 213434; Fax: 01 – 6476843 or 094 - 9378964
or through any bookseller

Text and drawings by: Gerard Lynch, Susan Roundtree, Shaffrey Associates Architects
Contributors: Brian Crowe, Pat McAfee
Series Editor: Jacqui Donnelly

Copy Editor: Eleanor Flegg
Design: Bennis Design

Contents

Introduction

The character of many of our historic buildings owes much to the quality of their brickwork. Fired ceramic brick has been used in Ireland since the sixteenth century and is a versatile, attractive, and durable material requiring no surface sealants and minimal maintenance. Brickwork is well suited to the Irish climate; it ages well, mellowing in colour over time, and will last for centuries, provided it has been properly made, detailed, and laid.

Most brick found in historic Irish buildings is of local origin. Brickmaking skills were developed in Ireland during the sixteenth and seventeenth centuries, and bricks were made from local clays in all parts of the country until well into the twentieth century and are still manufactured in some places today. Bricks were (and still are) also imported, particularly machine-made brick in the latter half of the nineteenth century. However, historically, transport and cost factors generally confined the use of imported material to façades and the parts of buildings that could be seen. During the eighteenth and nineteenth centuries, brick became the material of choice for constructing and facing buildings in Dublin and other coastal cities and towns. In inland areas, brick was used in combination with stone for lining walls, forming openings, vaulting, and in chimney and fireplace construction. Brick is still manufactured in Ireland and both home-produced and imported brick remain popular materials for facing buildings in the twenty-first century.

The repair of historic brickwork is a specialist area. While brick is generally very robust, it can be damaged by inappropriate repairs – such as badly specified or poorly executed repointing or cleaning. It can also fail if it is subject to excessive and on-going saturation with water. This booklet seeks to offer practical advice on how to inspect, maintain, and repair historic brickwork to ensure its continued well-being. Regular maintenance and correct repair will extend the life of any building and attending to minor defects as they arise makes sound economic sense.

In order to make informed decisions on how and when to repair historic brickwork, it is essential to understand and analyse the qualities of the brickwork in question. Until the latter years of the nineteenth century, brick in Ireland was hand-moulded. Traditionally-made bricks can be more fragile than their machine-made counterparts, and therefore easier to damage by inappropriate materials and techniques used in repair, repointing, and cleaning. When traditionally constructed brickwork is in need of repair, the work needs to be guided by good conservation principles. These should be balanced with a well-considered approach to the unique set of circumstances that each individual building and its brickwork problems will present. The final decision on repair should be the best possible, yet least intrusive, solution and one that will not cause damage in the long-term.

The beauty and versatility of brick have made it a popular construction material in Ireland, and throughout the world, for many hundreds of years

1. A Short History of Irish Brickwork

The origins of brickmaking

The use of clay brick for masonry structures dates back many thousands of years to the sun-baked bricks of the Far East, Africa, and South America. The process of burning, or firing, bricks to produce a stronger and more durable material was a later development that spread through Europe under the influence of the Romans. Fired brick was introduced into Britain through the conquering Roman legions around 2,000 years ago, but there is no evidence that brick was used in Ireland at that time. Brickmaking declined across Europe after the collapse of the Roman Empire, although bricks continued in use around the Mediterranean. The fashionable use of brick revived in later medieval times, particularly in northern Europe, and came to Britain during the fifteenth century, spreading from the south-east, where there was limited building stone, to other parts of Britain. Ireland, which had abundant resources of building stone, was slower to take up the practice of brickmaking. It was not until the middle of the sixteenth century that the first records exist for its manufacture and use.

RAW MATERIALS

Handmade bricks are normally made from the topmost, post-glacial surface deposits, brick earths, and clays. Up until the nineteenth century, bricks were usually made from boulder clay, mud, and silt deposited in and around lakes, rivers, and estuaries during the Pleistocene and Holocene Eras. The development of mechanisation in the nineteenth century allowed for the excavation of older, deeper, and harder clays and shales: those deposited at least 35 million years ago in the Eocene, Cretaceous, Jurassic, Triassic, and Carboniferous Eras. The individual nature of these materials influenced both the process of manufacture, and drying and firing methods. The raw material was excavated, ground, and prepared for particular moulding processes – such as machine-pressed or extruded wire-cut bricks.

MOULDING AND DRYING

Moulding and drying was originally a seasonal activity. The clay was excavated in the autumn and left exposed to weather naturally during the winter months. Rain, snow, and frost broke down the clay, washing out unwelcome natural salts. The following spring, the weathered clay was prepared for moulding. It was delivered to the handmoulder, who rolled a selected quantity to shape and then threw (or cast) it down hard into a timber mould, which had been dampened and sanded to aid release. The excess clay sticking out of the top of the mould was trimmed off and removed before the green (unfired) brick was taken away for drying. The green bricks were initially laid out flat on the ground and turned over frequently, or later stacked loosely in rows to dry for several weeks before firing. Both these processes took place in an area called the 'hackstead'. With mechanisation came controlled, heated drying rooms that allowed brickmaking to take place all year round and speeded up the process, producing a more consistent and controllable quality in the final brick.

FIRING THE BRICKS

Once fully dry the bricks were fired – the mineralogical content of the clay, the firing temperature, and the level of oxygen all influencing the final brick colour. The earliest method of firing was within temporary clamps consisting of layers of green bricks carefully arranged on a prepared base of parallel fire channels (or tunnels) formed with previously fired bricks. The outside of the clamp was then plastered with mud and the kiln set alight using brush or firewood, turf, coal, or culm as fuel in the tunnels. Later clamps, which used coal, did away with the fire channels and just had a base of coal across the length and width of the clamp. The firing took between several days and several weeks, depending on the size of the clamp. Once the fire was out and the clamp cooled, it was disassembled. The bricks produced varied in quality, depending on their position in the clamp, and had to be graded for use. Although this process produced a lot of waste bricks, a particularly large clamp could contain over a million bricks and was ideal for use where demand was intermittent and large numbers of bricks were needed seasonally.

Moulding

Drying

Firing

The process of making bricks by hand is still carried out in many countries. These images were taken in India and show moulding, drying and firing in clamp kilns

KILNS

Kilns were permanent structures which, until the nineteenth century, had to be loaded (or set), fired, cooled, and un-loaded before they could be set and fired again. These are known as intermittent kilns. The first were updraught kilns, wasteful of fuel, where the fire was lit at the base, travelled up through the bricks and tiles, and exited at the top. By the middle of the nineteenth century the more efficient downdraught kiln was developed, whereby the heat was drawn over the top and down through the goods. This gave greater control and improved the quality and regular colour of the bricks. The second half of the nineteenth century saw the introduction of continuous kilns, where the fire travelling through the kiln never goes out. The bricks go through the pre-heating, firing, cooling and unloading processes in separate but interconnected chambers. The first was the 'Hoffmann Kiln' patented by Friedrich Hoffmann in 1856. Modern continuous kilns include the 'tunnel' kiln, where the bricks travel on rails through all the zones, or the 'moving-hood' kiln, which is brought to, and lowered over, the setting of bricks and then ignited.

A kiln chimney at Youghal, Co. Cork, now disused

Early Irish brickwork

The earliest known use of clay brick in Irish buildings dates to the sixteenth century, when it was used in prominent buildings such as Ormond Castle, County Tipperary, and Bunratty Castle, County Clare. A written record exists for the manufacture of brick in County Wexford in 1551-2, while the earliest reference to brickmaking in Dublin is in the administrative records of the city in 1599. Brick use is recorded in some houses and chimneys of the sixteenth century and is indicated in a view of Trinity College, dated 1591. In Ulster its use is closely associated with the Plantation dwellings of the early seventeenth century. Preparation and assembly of materials on site, including brick, is recorded in early seventeenth-century surveys of Plantation properties, including Captain Nicholas Pynnar's survey of 1611. Brick itself exists in a few surviving buildings from this time, generally in small quantities associated with fireplaces, chimneys, ovens, and pistol loops.

Jigginstown House, Naas, Co. Kildare, built c.1637-40, is the first Irish building where imported brick and bricklaying expertise are believed to have been used although the majority of the bricks are thought to be of local origin

Mountjoy Fort, Co. Tyrone, built c.1603, is the earliest known surviving Irish building where brick was used as the substantive building material for walls

Jigginstown House (c.1637-1640) in Naas, County Kildare, was a high status building erected by Thomas Wentworth, Lord Lieutenant of Ireland, at a cost of £6,000. It is of major significance as an early brick building in Ireland and set the fashion for building country mansions in brick; including later seventeenth-century houses such as Burton, County Cork, and Blessington, County Wicklow (although neither survives).

Bricks were generally made locally at this time, or on the site of the building. This practice continued in rural areas into the eighteenth century, although there were commercial brickfields in the major cities. Early seventeenth-century bricks were generally longer and thinner than later bricks.

Early descriptions of brickmaking in Ireland are rare, probably because it was craft based; an expertise handed down by practice. Gerard Boate's description of brickmaking in his book *Ireland's Natural History* (1652) is, therefore, very useful, although evidence now shows him to have been somewhat inaccurate in his assertion that brick was not much used in Ireland before then. Similarly, the Civil Survey of 1654 also does not indicate widespread use of brick, but it is known from other sources that brick was being used nationally for minor purposes at that time although not necessarily as a substantive building material. After the Great Fire of London in 1666, legislation was enacted for the use of brick in buildings, and banning timber as a major structural or facing element.

The effects of this legislation were also seen in Ireland, where building leases for St Stephen's Green, Dublin, specified the houses to be built with brick or stone. An increasing number of brickmakers and bricklayers are recorded in Dublin in the period after 1660, and the presence of city brickfields indicates that brick was being used to build both public and private buildings by the close of the seventeenth century.

Georgian brickwork

The use of brick as a material suitable for buildings of high architectural quality was considerably enhanced in the early eighteenth century by the work of Edward Lovett Pearce (1699-1733), Surveyor General, and Ireland's most important architect of the period. His confident use of brick was influenced by his travels and knowledge of brick buildings in Italy and the Netherlands. He was also author, in 1730, of the first Irish Act of Parliament (3 Geo.II. c.14) that incorporated quality control measures for brickmaking. It also specified a size for bricks made for commercial purposes in Ireland, although interestingly, the bricks found in Irish buildings of this time are not generally of the specified dimensions.

The brick façade, with stone dressings, of Cashel Palace, Co. Tipperary, was designed by Edward Lovett Pearce before 1729 for Archbishop Goodwin

The use of brick in country houses by Richard Castle (1695-1751) and other eighteenth-century architects provides important evidence of its acceptance countrywide, and confirms that the material and expertise required to manufacture bricks were available across eighteenth-century Ireland. These buildings also demonstrate construction detailing with brick, such as brick vaulting, a most useful technique for structural support work, building without timber (other than for temporary centring or

support), and providing enhanced fireproofing. There are examples of the use of brick in many eighteenth-century landscape and garden structures throughout the country. These include pigeon houses, granaries and barns, garden walls, icehouses, gazebos, summer houses, temples, towers, and mausolea.

Ruined garden house of brick at Newbridge House Demesne, Co. Dublin

Garden walls lined with brick at Beaulieu House, Co. Louth. The orientation of garden walls was the subject of several gardening manuals in the early eighteenth century. The recommendations were that walls should face south-east, south-west, north-east and north-west. The first two, for example, were considered good for best fruit; the latter for plums, cherries and baking pears

The brick façades of Irish buildings in the eighteenth century were not subject to the same rapidly changing fashions as those in Britain. Locally produced bricks were limited in quality and the fine bricks needed to execute gauged (or rubbed) brickwork for fine architectural dressings had to be imported. In Ireland in the seventeenth and eighteenth centuries, the evidence for gauged work other than simple arches seems to be limited to a few high-status buildings. Similarly, the colour of brick façades appears unrelated to London fashions and had more to do with the natural brick colours resulting from the firing of available local clays. Red was the most popular colour for brickwork throughout the eighteenth and early nineteenth centuries. In Dublin there is evidence that some red brick was imported but also that the local 'grey' (buff) brick was used and coloured red, using a naturally pigmented Venetian Red wash.

Although many surviving minor buildings show the use of crudely-made brick, it was generally too expensive for houses of the poor, except where philanthropic landlords carried out housing improvements.

Dublin brickfields are noted in some early eighteenth-century deeds and on mid-century maps of the city, and the names of certain brickmakers are identified in connection with the Merrion Brickfields. In the 1770s, legislation banning brickmaking in the cities of Dublin and Cork for health reasons resulted in the development of new brickfields in areas outside the cities. Brickmaking sites adjacent to canals were convenient for transporting the fuels necessary for firing (primarily turf and culm), as well as for distributing the finished bricks. Sources of clay for brickmaking were also, where possible, exploited whilst the canals were excavated.

The evidence of widespread brickmaking in Ireland is clear from several sources, including early maps. Examination of official importation records, such as the Irish Export Import Records indicates that the quantities of brick imported were relatively small, and less significant than previously believed. It is interesting to note that more brick was imported into Cork than into Dublin in the eighteenth century. Importation figures generally rose towards the end of the eighteenth century because of the increase in building activity and the removal of the city brickfields. Imported brick, however, was more expensive than the local product and is therefore likely to have been used sparingly. Most imported brick came from England although some came from Holland. Architect George Wilkinson (writing about available building materials in 1845) refers to the use of imported Bridgwater (Somerset) brick in Dublin. Generally, English handmade imported brick appears very similar to the native material and thus is difficult to identify visually.

Nineteenth century brick

Brickfields established in the most remote locations of every county indicate just how widely brick was used during the nineteenth century in all kinds of buildings. The importance of convenient transport for the industry is underlined by the fact that many brickfields were located adjacent to navigable waterways, estuaries, and rivers. By the early nineteenth century there was significant trade in brick along the canals, signifying brickmaking activity in the midlands, particularly around Tullamore and Athy.

Groom's Cottage, Monasterevan, Co. Kildare, c.1882 constructed of machine-made red brick from Kingscourt, Co. Cavan and hand-made yellow brick from Athy, Co. Kildare

The mechanisation of brickmaking was late in coming to Ireland, although incentives to improve the quality of Irish brick had existed from the mid-eighteenth century through premiums offered by the Dublin Society. The Irish products shown at the 1853 Industrial Exhibition in Dublin reveal the interest shown by native brick producers at that time; even though very few Irish brickmakers took part in the exhibition. This was probably because most brickmaking operations were local craft-based practices without the financial means to develop into more highly industrialised processes. Study of the exhibition catalogue provides valuable information about the range of machines that could then be employed in brickmaking, based primarily on experience in England where the mechanised process was well underway.

The Red Stables, St Anne's Park, Raheny, Dublin, built in 1886 of machine-made brick from the Portmarnock Brickworks

As in England, the development of the rail network ensured the reliable, cheap transportation of bricks to all parts of the country. This had a significant effect on the establishment, or enlargement, of Irish brickmaking companies. These new companies did not, however, take business away from the more traditional brickmaking areas. The production of handmade bricks remained stable during this period and well into the early twentieth century. What the new companies did attempt to do was to try to compete with imported bricks.

Twentieth century to the present

Despite their best efforts, Irish manufacturers simply could not keep up with demand for bricks of the overall consistency of quality, range, and types that could be imported. The advent of autoclaved (as opposed to kiln-fired) bricks made of concrete and calcium silicate (sand-lime) in the early twentieth century, though very small in production compared with clay bricks, had a further negative effect on market share, and thus the economies, of these companies. Radical changes in construction materials and methods, as well as politics, also played a part in the demise of the traditional brickmakers employing hand-moulding techniques in Ireland. Today there are only four brickmaking plants on the island of Ireland, each producing machine-made facing bricks in modern metric sizes. Despite a long and relatively successful brickmaking history in Ireland, the range of different types of handmade facing bricks in imperial sizes needed for repairing historic buildings now have to be imported specifically for that purpose.

An interesting use of brick in Dublin from 1930s: Chancery House designed by Herbert Simms, chief housing architect, Dublin Corporation

Conservation principles

In a sense, we look after our historic buildings for those who come after us. Many of these buildings have been around for generations before us and it is our responsibility to hand them on in good condition to allow future generations to enjoy them too. In order that the works you undertake do not damage the special qualities of a historic building, it is important to understand some of the basic principles of good building conservation. Many of these are common-sense and all are based on an understanding of how old buildings work and how, with sensitive treatment, they can stay special.

Before you start, learn as much as you can about your particular building. What is its history? How has it changed over time? Remember that later alterations may be important too and evidence that the building has been cared for and adapted over the years with each generation adding its own layer to a unique history.

CARRYING OUT MAINTENANCE OR REPAIR WORKS

> Do use the acknowledged experts - get independent and objective advice from the right people and only employ skilled craft workers with proven experience in the type of work required

> Do repair the parts of the building that need it - do not replace them unless they can no longer do the job they were designed to do

> Do make sure the right materials and repair techniques are used and that even the smallest changes you make to the building are done well

> Do use techniques that can be easily reversed or undone. This allows for any unforeseen problems to be corrected in future without damage to the special qualities of the building

> Do establish and understand the reasons for failure before undertaking repairs

> Do record all repair works for the benefit of future owners

> Don't overdo it – only do as much work to the building as is necessary, and as little as possible

> Don't look at problems in isolation – consider them in the context of the building as a whole

> Don't use architectural salvage from elsewhere unless you are certain that the taking of the materials hasn't caused the destruction of other old buildings or been the result of theft

Getting the right advice

When it comes to repairing a building, regardless of its age or size, it is important to know when specialist advice is needed and where to find the right help. It is a false economy not to get the best advice before having work carried out. Bad repair works can be difficult and expensive to undo. They can damage a building in the long-term and devalue your property.

You will need the right advice for a particular job. Sometimes you will require a craftsman, or an architect, a surveyor or a structural engineer. Sometimes you will need specialist advice from someone with a particular expertise, perhaps to analyse a lime mortar or advise on cleaning techniques. At the outset, and particularly if your building is a protected structure, you may need advice on whether the proposed works require planning permission or not. When undertaking a large or complex conservation and repair project, a multi-disciplinary team may be required. Most importantly, you should ensure that any adviser is independent and objective. Avoid taking advice from someone trying to sell you something, or someone with a vested interest in increasing the scale and expense of work. Many building professionals and contractors are principally involved with modern construction and may not know how to deal sympathetically with an old building. You need someone who understands old buildings, has experience in dealing with them, and has trained to work with them. He or she should be knowledgeable and have experience in dealing with your type of building.

When employing a professional adviser or a building contractor, check their qualifications and status with the relevant bodies and institutes. Ask for references, and for the locations and photographs of recent similar work undertaken. Do not be afraid to follow up references and to visit other building projects. A good practitioner will not mind you doing this. If you see a good job successfully completed on a building similar to yours, find out who did the work, whether they would be suitable for the works you want to undertake, and if the building owner was satisfied.

Try to get at least three written estimates or quotations for the work from suitable contractors. Do not make your final choice based on cost alone. The cheapest quote you receive may be from a person who does not fully understand the complexity of the problem. Do not make payments for work until you are satisfied it has been correctly completed.

Be clear when briefing your adviser about what you want him or her to do. A good adviser should be able to undertake an inspection of your property, give you a report identifying the causes of damage, make a careful diagnosis of the problem, recommend repairs, specify the work required, get a firm price from a suitable builder or craftsman, and oversee the work on site as it progresses. If your building is likely to need ongoing works over a number of years, your relationship with your adviser and builder will be important both to you and your building, and continuity will be a great advantage. They will be able to become familiar with the property, and to understand how it acts, and will build up expertise based on your particular building.

The Royal Institute of the Architects of Ireland (RIAI) has an accreditation system for architects trained in building conservation and can provide a list of those architects that are accredited. The Irish Georgian Society maintains a register of practitioners known to have some traditional building and conservation skills. The Construction Industry Federation also has a register of Heritage Contractors working in the field of building conservation. The conservation officer in your local authority can provide general advice and may be able to recommend suitable professionals, craft workers and suppliers in your area.

2. Understanding Historic Brickwork

This section gives an overview of the typical historic brickwork found in Irish buildings. It covers the survey of brickwork: identifying types, colour and sizes of brick and the construction methods used, as well as bonding patterns of brickwork; varieties of pointing and jointing methods; mortars and finishes; the different building elements for which brick was used; decorative brickwork; and other fired earth products including terracotta, faïence and stoneware.

Rathmines Library, Dublin, opened 1913, constructed of Arklow brick and terracotta designed to resemble stonework

Balbriggan Library, Co. Dublin, opened 1906, constructed of Portmarnock brick

The types and qualities of brick earth and clay suitable for brickmaking are widespread and varied. Almost any type can be used but some can be problematic, for example, those containing an excess of lime inclusions in the clay. Many of the problems associated with the quality of Irish brick stem from the clay preparation techniques. Excess lime becomes reactive quicklime during firing, and slaking on contact with moisture leads to its expansion and spalling of parts of the brick face. This was frequently blamed for the poor quality of Irish brick. It is also possible that some of the problems encountered were to do with natural salt content of the clays, as many eighteenth- and early nineteenth-century sites were associated with estuaries, or in the case of Dublin, with the strands on either side of the port of Dublin.

Brickmaking carried out in the midlands does not seem to have come in for the same amount of criticism. Bricks from Athy, County Kildare, and Tullamore, County Offaly, for example, were very well regarded in the nineteenth century. Brickmaking descriptions, such as those that survive from Gillen, County Offaly, Glenmore, County Kilkenny, and Athy, County Kildare, are important and rare accounts of a now obsolete process, rarely mentioned in folklore. Until the 1930s, most bricks were laid in soft and flexible lime-based mortars in solid thick-walled construction that relied on mass for stability. From this period onwards, cavity wall masonry set with hard and rigid cement-based mortars became the established method of brickwork construction.

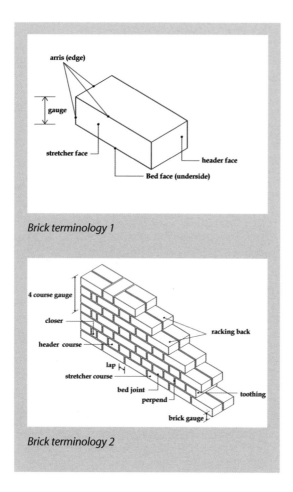

Brick terminology 1

Brick terminology 2

Machine-made brick from the Dolphin's Barn Factory in Crumlin dating from the early twentieth century is recognisable from its distinctive yellow colouring and the manufacturer's name impressed into the 'frog' or indentation in the bed face of the brick

Types of brick

The types of brick found in Irish buildings fall into two main categories: they are either handmade or machine-made.

Handmade bricks were, as the name suggests, moulded in individual boxes by hand, dried, and then fired either in temporary clamp kilns or permanent kiln structures. All traditionally made bricks were graded, according to their suitability for use, into three main types. The best bricks were selected for facing work. In Ireland, these were generally described as stock or facing bricks. General brick suitable for building work but not for facing brickwork was called place brick or common brick. The rest of the bricks from the kiln were either over-burnt and misshapen (clinkers) or under-burnt and were generally unusable for anything other than rough or non-structural work.

Machine-made bricks are those made by a mechanised process, such as an extruded 'wirecut', pressed and 'simulated' handmade. Machine-made bricks can be solid, perforated, or panelled and are often stamped with the maker's name.

RUBBERS AND CUTTERS

These are special, high quality bricks made from top-most silica-bearing brick earth or clay. They are low-fired, or baked, to a point just short of chemical change or vitrification. This creates a soft textured brick, yet one that is strong enough to be cut and rubbed for some types of highly-skilled ornate work, such as moulded cornices and string courses, architraves, columns and arches; and capable of good weathering provided the work is properly detailed. Since the late nineteenth century, rubbers were often made oversized to allow for cutting to shape in a shaped box using a bow saw fitted with a twisted wire blade. As far as present research suggests, these were never produced in Ireland.

ENGINEERING BRICKS

These bricks are manufactured from a natural deposit of a clay type that, when fully fired, naturally creates a strong, dense, non-porous and generally smooth, blue or red coloured, face. Their popular use developed in the nineteenth century for civil engineering applications such as bridges, viaducts, platforms, and tunnels. They were also used in domestic and small-scale buildings for aesthetic reasons where their colour gave a visual contrast with the general bricks used.

GLAZED BRICKS

The early glazing of bricks came about as a direct result of the combination of wood fires and high temperatures against the face of the bricks in the firing tunnels. These bricks were then used to create decorative patterns within a brick wall, including diaper work. Later glazed bricks were machine-made, usually with one glazed surface. The earliest were termed 'salt-glazed' and were generally brown in colour. Later developments in the mid nineteenth century led to the fired brick being dipped into a prepared solution of liquid clay. This was usually white, but could be pigmented to create a wide range of colours and then re-fired at a higher temperature. Glazed bricks were often used, because of their light-reflecting and self-cleansing qualities, on shop fronts, toilets, dairies, and light wells in the nineteenth and early twentieth century buildings.

Glazed bricks, in white or pale colours, were often used to the sides of windows and in light wells to reflect more light into the interior of a building

CONCRETE AND CALCIUM SILICATE (SAND-LIME) BRICKS

Unlike clay bricks fired in a kiln, these bricks are cast in moulds, using aggregate physically bound by either cement or lime and then hardened in a steam-heated autoclave and left to cure. First invented and patented in Great Britain in 1866, they were commercially developed in Germany at the end of the nineteenth century, although large scale production really only began in the early twentieth century.

Historic sizes of Irish bricks

Size and visual appearance can give some assistance in dating bricks, particularly those made in the period before bricks were machine-made and stamped. Due to the nature of early moulding, bricks were generally thin in the medieval period and gradually became thicker, with improved moulding techniques, during the seventeenth century.

The changing sizes of brick: this image shows, from the top, the thin bricks of the seventeenth century, an eighteenth-century handmade brick and a nineteenth-century machine-made brick

In Ireland, brick size was guided by legislation passed in 1730, based on practical matters such as a sensible size and weight for bricklayers to easily manipulate with one hand while holding a trowel with the other, and all-round proportions relating to the accurate bonding of each brick to one another. Handmade bricks could vary significantly in dimensions and there is much local variation – the so-called 'canal' bricks brought into Dublin from places along the canal routes are noted to be smaller than those produced elsewhere.

The minimum size stipulated by the Act of Parliament of 1730 was 9½" x 4½" x 2¼", an unusual choice, being larger than the contemporary English Statute sizes (largely relating to London) or the size of brick then in general use in Dublin either at that time or later. It seems to have been largely ignored. In 1816 the Corporation of Bricklayers and Plasterers said that, in the previous year, the magistrates had to choose between suspending the Act and putting a sudden stop to all building in Dublin, because no bricks being used were of that Statute size.

Notable historic brick sizes recorded in Ireland

Seventeenth century bricks (before 1660): between 8½-9¾ x 4-4⅝ x 1¾-2⅝ inches

Eighteenth century bricks (1730 Act): 9½ x 4½ x 2¼ inches

Eighteenth century bricks (more typical size): 9 x 4½ x 2½ inches

Nineteenth century 'canal' bricks: 8½ x 3¾ x 2¾ inches

Nineteenth century machine-made bricks: 9 x 4½ x 2¾ inches

BS Imperial Bricks: 8⅝ x 4⅛ x 2⅝ inches (UK 1965)

Modern metric-sized bricks (I.S. 91): 215 x 102.5 x 65mm

Handmade bricks can be challenging to build with because of their irregularity in size and shape; particularly for the modern bricklayer, tutored and experienced in the use of regular, machine-made bricks. From a historic building perspective, handmade bricks have a unique value that later mechanised counterparts fired in modern computer controlled, gas or oil-fired, kilns simply cannot replicate. The variation in colour and surface texture was a product of the handmade brickmaking process, as well as traditional fuels and methods of firing.

Traditional brick bonding

The way that bricks are arranged, or bonded, in walls has a direct relationship with the construction method employed. In modern buildings with cavity walls, bricks are usually built in what is called 'stretcher' bond, where only the long faces of the bricks are visible. This type of wall is also called a 'half-brick' wall because the thickness of the wall is only the thickness of a brick width, which is half the length of a brick.

In historic buildings with solid walls most brickwork is constructed as at least one brick thick – that is the thickness of the wall is equivalent to the length, or stretcher, of a full brick. However, everything may not be as it seems as on the façades of many cavity walled buildings bricklayers often deliberately cut, or 'snap', a brick in two in order to lay them to appear as headers and create the appearance of the more familiar, and more attractive, traditional solid wall construction. These shortened bricks are known as snapped headers.

English bond, Flemish bond, and variations of these, are the most frequently seen bonding patterns. English bond, of alternating courses of stretchers and headers, is structurally the strongest brick bond. Early examples of English bond are rare in Ireland. There are examples at Mountjoy Castle, County Tyrone, and at Jigginstown House, County Kildare. There was, however, a revival in the use of English bond in the early years of the twentieth century. English Garden Wall bond is a variation of English bond, having three or five courses of stretchers to one course of headers.

Flemish bond, of alternating stretchers and headers in the same course, became popular in Ireland in the seventeenth century. At the time it was perceived to be more attractive in appearance than what had by then become known as 'Old English' bond. Flemish bond, although less strong than English bond, became very fashionable and was used in most Irish buildings of the eighteenth and nineteenth centuries.

By the Georgian period, it had become a popular bricklaying practice to use selected first class bricks for fronting the outer face of the main façade. These 'fronts' were often only randomly bonded into the brick wall behind because a proportion of the headers could be gained by cutting two faces from one brick. Flemish bond was particularly suited to this practice, especially when an expensive (or imported) front brick was used. The subsequent lack of tying-in full (or through) headers into the backing brickwork can be a cause of significant structural problems. (See Chapter 3)

Common brick bonding patterns

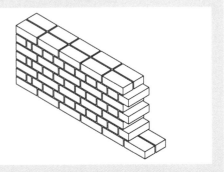

English bond – commonly used on seventeenth buildings until overtaken by Flemish bond brickwork; its use was revived in the late-nineteenth century

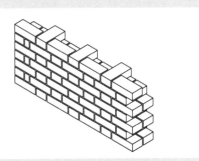

Flemish bond - commonly used on late-seventeenth to early twentieth-century buildings

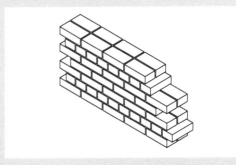

English Garden Wall bond – commonly used on early twentieth-century buildings

Stretcher bond – used on buildings from the 1930s onwards

Historic brick colours

In London, the colour of brick used in façades was subject firstly to clay type and manufacturing methods, and secondly to fashion and taste. After the 1730s red bricks declined in popularity in favour of more subtle buff colours. Isaac Ware, in his *Complete Body of Architecture* (1756), describes the mid-century change of taste in England from 'hot' to 'cool' brick colours, red being considered *'too fiery and disagreeable to the eye'*. In Ireland, however, perhaps due to the smaller range of the clay types available, red remained the fashionable colour for façade brickwork. Even in the nineteenth century, when buff coloured bricks were available in Ireland, red bricks seem to have been the most popular, but local brickmaking enterprises were not always able to produce such a colour in sufficient quantity to satisfy the market. It became fashionable to colour façades with a Venetian Red colour wash (not lime wash).

Colour-washed façade brickwork can be seen to the building on the left

COLOUR WASHING

Colour washing of the brickwork of the principal façades was common practice in Ireland, and was used from the seventeenth century onwards. This practice was also known as 'raddling' or 'ruddling'. It was primarily used to regularise the varying tones of clamp-fired and early kiln-fired bricks. It also gave a small degree of protection to soft handmade bricks and slow-setting lime mortars.

Colour washes were made using natural ochres, combined with glue size and a fixative such as alum or copperas. Generally colour washing was also historically combined with white painted lines, termed 'pencilling', made of distemper (a mix of crushed chalk and glue size) applied over part of the ochred joints in order to re-define them, but to a lesser scale. This can be seen in the fine eighteenth-century brickwork ruins of The Hellfire Club at Desmond's Castle, Askeaton, County Limerick.

Colour washed bricks with traces of pencilling to the joints at the Hell Fire Club, Desmond's Castle, Askeaton, Co. Limerick

Traditional lime mortars and bedding materials

The materials used in brickwork joints are very significant as the joints can typically form 20% and up to 30% of the overall surface area of a wall. The lime mortar joint system acts as a flexible gasket in thick walled construction and is the conduit through which the masonry is able to breathe and accommodate normal thermal movement. The process of finishing the bedding mortar to a variety of profiles is called 'jointing'. The term 'pointing' is used when a later,

usually more refined, separate mortar is applied onto the bedding mortar and brought to the desired profile.

In most historic thick-walled masonry construction the pointing and bedding mortars were lime-based. These mortars complemented the original stones or bricks and did not restrict moisture and thermal movement. To undertake repairs, repointing, and re-construction of historic brickwork, the selection of the correct class of lime, associated materials (such as, aggregates, water, pigments and pozzolans), and their ratio to one another, are absolutely crucial.

Recent repointing of a brick wall with a lime-based mortar

Historic jointing and pointing styles

Historically, there were a number of different ways a bricklayer could finish the mortar joints between the bricks, and many of these methods required a high level of skill and craftsmanship. It is important to take note of the way the brickwork joints were finished as this contributes greatly to the character of the whole wall. Brickwork in rear and side walls was generally simply jointed with no separate pointing process. The most common joint finishes found on historic brick buildings in Ireland vary according to brick type as follows:

Common styles of joint profiles found in historic brickwork:

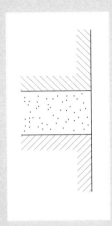

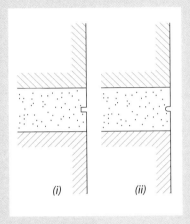

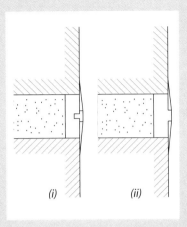

Flush joints

Ruled joints

This joint profile is found on historic buildings as a square (i) or rounded (ii) profile

Wigged joints

This is possibly an Irish derivation of bastard tuck pointing. The tuck may have been formed as a ribbon as in bastard tuck pointing technique (i) or formed out of the stopping mortar (ii). These drawings are based on examined samples of historic wigging

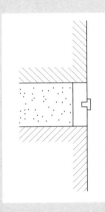

Bastard tuck joints

The joint is finished flush with the brick face and cut top and bottom and the cuts can vary in width and profile. Sometimes the façade is colour washed and pencilled. In an Irish context, this technique can also be referred to as ruled top and bottom and/or double struck

Tuck pointed joints

This pointing technique is carried out in a number of stages. A coloured stopping mortar is applied and then grooved to receive a later application of the tuck

Struck joints

With the advent of the weather-struck and cut profile, this style became more commonly known as overhand struck

Weather-struck and cut joints

FLUSH POINTING

These joints are generally plain and finished flush and flat to the wall face with a trowel as the walling is constructed. From the early seventeenth century onwards, the joints could also be lightly grooved, or ruled using a thin-bladed instrument called a jointer to the centre of the horizontal and vertical joints, guided level and plumb, by the timber pointing-rule or feather edge.

RULED POINTING

Ruled joints are flush joints which are then cut by running a thin-bladed instrument called a jointer along the centre of the joints, guided level and plumb by the use of a pointing rule, to ensure a level and plumb profile. This finish is also called by the later terms 'penny-round' or 'joints-jointed'. On some historic brickwork, after the façade was colour washed, the groove was highlighted with a painted white line of distemper in a process termed pencilling.

Ruling was, and is, NEVER executed with the blade of a trowel, as this would only slice, not joint, the face of the joints.

WIGGING (IRISH TUCK POINTING)

The technique traditionally known as wigging is based on the long-established methods of bastard tuck jointing or pointing. In conjunction with the colour washing of façades, the wigging technique was also used in repointing to improve the appearance of poor quality brick in the nineteenth century.

Wigging is executed with an un-pigmented lime mortar joint in one of several ways. It can be carried out by skilfully trimming away of some of the fine bedding mortar either side to create a ribbon. Alternatively, in a manner like true tuck pointing, it can be applied in a separate operation onto the grooved base mortar, but using the same mortar mix and then skilfully trimmed with a sharp knife called a Frenchman, guided along a carefully positioned timber pointing rule, or feather-edge, to leave a slightly raised ribbon in the centre of the joint. The rest of the joint is then 'wigged' by applying a thin layer of brick-coloured mortar containing natural pigment, such as Venetian Red.

Wigging in its weathered state gives building façades a very particular appearance. In conservation work, this can present difficult choices. Most contractors today are unfamiliar with this pointing style and

consequently façades are usually repointed either with plain joints, or else traditionally tuck pointed and almost all are executed with a much heavier hand and whiter mortar than originally intended. This can dramatically alter the appearance and character of the original building façade.

The preparation of a sample of wigging repair

i)   creating the bastard tuck profile

ii)   laying in the pigmented stopping mortar up to the ribbon

iii)   the finished wigging sample

TUCK POINTING

This style of jointing is predominantly seen used on English brickwork from the late seventeenth century and it continued in popular use there throughout the eighteenth, nineteenth, and early twentieth centuries. It can be seen in the interior of the nineteenth century church in Eyrecourt, Co. Galway.

Tuck pointing, done properly, is the most highly skilled of all pointing finishes. It was introduced to give the illusion of finely jointed gauged brickwork on some principal façades. The effect was achieved by pigmenting the pointing mortar to match the colour-washed facing brick. Over this a narrow ribbon of fine, generally white or cream coloured, pointing material of well-sifted lime mixed with fine silica sand, is skilfully applied, or 'tucked', onto the regularly grooved centres of the prepared joints and precisely trimmed to size. Historically, the stopping mortar was applied thinly to still-green bedding mortar in contrast to modern repointing where a more substantial key is usually specified.

Tuck pointing has recently become popular in Ireland as a repointing technique for the façades of buildings that should more properly be repointed in the original wigging style.

Tuck pointing in practice

Façade with historic wigged brickwork

STRUCK

This is one of the oldest and most subtle jointing profiles which, when properly executed, survives well. Also known as 'reverse struck' or 'overhand-struck'.

WEATHER-STRUCK AND CUT

This is a nineteenth-century pointing profile in which the joint is formed by the bricklayer compressing the top portion of the joint back more than the lower, inclining the blade as he finishes the joint in one stroke. The lower edge is then trimmed level to the arris of the brick with the Frenchman run along the pointing rule. The vertical joints are sloped left to right, which is the opposite of the struck profile. This joint is over-used as a profile, outside of its historical period of use, on repointing of historic brickwork, and is often poorly executed, in a heavy-handed manner; unlike the more subtle original technique.

RECESSED

The use of slightly recessed flush joints can be found in buildings built with machine-made brick in the twentieth century.

Use of cement in historic mortars

Using an inappropriate rigid material, like cement, to repair, repoint, or rebuild a wall that was originally built with lime-based mortar will lead to long-term problems with the individual softer bricks and the overall masonry. Too rigid a joint will not allow either for thermal movement or the movement of moisture in the wall, and can cause cracking and decay of masonry.

Artificial cements were invented in the early-nineteenth century. The best known of these is Portland cement, invented by a bricklayer, Joseph Aspdin, who patented the process for its manufacture in 1824. Since then, artificial cements have been consistently developed to improve their quality in terms of speed of set, ultimate strength, and consistency of performance to meet building standards. It is important to understand, however, that due to the lower temperatures of earlier kilns and the inability to grind a dry-hydrate as finely as is possible today, the Ordinary Portland Cements manufactured up until the 1930s were nothing like the modern product; having about one-fifth of the compressive strength of their present counterparts.

Therefore, in replicating historic mortars known to have been based on specific cement : lime : sand ratios, it is vital to understand that they were much weaker than an equivalent mortar based on those ratios today and this should be taken into account in the design of the mortar.

Brick building elements

Most people are familiar with the use of brick in the external walls of buildings. But this versatile building material has been put to many other uses in construction each of which has its own specific issues regarding care and maintenance.

CHIMNEYS

One of the earliest uses of brick in Ireland was for ovens, fireplaces, and chimneys. As an already fired product with heat absorbing properties, brick was suitable for any location subject to extremes of heating and cooling. Using similarly shaped masonry units to construct a chimney was also undoubtedly easier than using irregular-shaped quarried stone. For these reasons, on many buildings of stone or mud-wall construction, the only externally visible brickwork feature will be the chimney. Chimneys are generally the most exposed parts of any building and have to cope with persistent wetting and drying, and heating and cooling cycles, as well as years of wind and frost action that all take their toll on the brickwork. In addition, the brickwork can suffer the chemical effects of the sulphurous by-products of coal fires.

Decorative polychromatic brick chimneys at Castlebellingham, Co. Louth

Many chimneys are decorative features in their own right and contribute to the particular character of the individual building or street. They give character to roofscapes and should always be retained in historic buildings unless there are very particular structural reasons not to do so.

WINDOW OPENINGS

It was accepted practice in the eighteenth and nineteenth centuries for openings within stone walls to be formed by brick, with brick relieving arches. A relieving arch is an arch built into the masonry wall above a window or door, which takes some of the loading off the lintel or arch directly above the opening. Generally these stone walls were rendered externally and the brickwork covered over. Brick surrounds, however, were sometimes highlighted in the architectural design and incorporated into façade ornamentation with other brick dressings such as string courses. John Semple, detailing his scheme for Public Offices in 1758, specifies that all the doors and chimneys are to have 9-inch (225mm) brick arches *'or discharging arches turned over or in them, as is usual, in the most lasting, and substantial buildings.'*

Eighteenth-century window heads, formed with brick, usually have flat or straight arches. Camber arches, with a very slight rise in the centre, are also found. In high quality work, low-fired and soft-textured bricks, termed 'rubbing bricks' or 'rubbers', were often selected for this purpose and skilfully 'cut and rubbed' to the established radial shape so as to fit neatly and accurately together as arch bricks (or voussoirs) set with very thin joints of fine lime-rich mortar. In Ireland, more usually, flat arches were built using ordinary bricks, cut to shape radially, or

A typical Irish eighteenth-century flat arch window head. It differs from similar English flat arches of the period in that the arch does not splay widely at either end

using pre-moulded voussoirs. Alternatively the bricks were laid uncut, relying on tapered joints to achieve the required curved and radial alignment.

The way in which window openings in Ireland differ in constructional quality and aesthetic appearance from those found, for example, in London, with infrequent use of 'cut and rubbed' or gauged brickwork, may be a result of the high costs involved in this type of brickwork. Window jambs, likewise, are rarely executed in gauged work in Ireland.

Early windows were usually set close to the face of the wall, with visible timber frames and sash boxes. These are still occasionally to be found in early eighteenth-century buildings. However, the 1730 Building Act decreed that window frames should be set back for a width of one brick into the reveal, and this gradually became standard practice.

In the early nineteenth century, a fashion developed, particularly in Dublin and Limerick, to apply a thin coating of painted lime plaster to the external brick reveals of window openings. These 'patent reveals' protected the brickwork reveals, and their junction with the timber window frame, from the elements and also reflected light into the rooms inside. In true patent reveals, the lime plaster tapers in thickness from the window frame out to the edge of the brickwork.

BRICK VAULTING

In Ireland the vaulting-off of basement floors in brick became an accepted form of construction from early in the seventeenth century. This is a very strong building form and can support heavy upper floor finishes, such as stone, marble slabs, bricks or thick clay tiles. The use of vaulting eliminated the need for timber construction at ground floor level. This was particularly advantageous for fire protection, as it separated potential sources of fire, such as kitchens and service areas in the basement, from the upper floors. In addition the qualities of the arched shape, combined with the overall thickness of the brick construction of the vaulting, provided useful sound proofing between floors.

Skilfully built (or 'turned') over a carefully positioned temporary timber framework (or 'centre') of suitable size, one of the earliest examples of ribbed vaulting, or cross vaulting in brick, is found in the undercroft of Jigginstown House. This general method of construction became more widely adopted during the eighteenth century; when most buildings with

The brick-vaulted undercroft of Jigginstown House, Co. Kildare

entrance hall floors of stone flags were supported on brick-vaulted basement chambers. Examples such as Ballyhaise (c.1733), County Cavan and the King House (c.1730), Boyle, County Roscommon, are unusual because they have all their floors vaulted in brick, probably for reasons of fire safety. Brick vaulting was also used in some stables and out-offices, such as those at Strokestown (c.1740), County Roscommon.

Even in buildings with walls entirely constructed of stone, such as the Royal Exchange (c.1770), now Dublin's City Hall, brick vaulting supports the upper ground floor. Other examples include the Parliament House (1729-1739), now the Bank of Ireland, College Green, designed by Edward Lovett Pearce, where the vaults beneath the building are constructed with brick. John Semple, in 1758, specifies brick vaulting as follows *'Both the stories of sd. four offices are to be groin'd, or vaulted with nine inch Brick arches.'*

One of the finest examples of the use of brick both for damp-proofing and fireproofing purposes – as well as to help contain any accidental explosion – is the original gunpowder magazine store in the Magazine Fort (1734) in the Phoenix Park. The walls are at least $2\frac{1}{2}$ feet (760mm) thick, finished externally with coursed limestone, but lined and vaulted with brick.

INTERNAL BRICKWORK

Internal walls of brick, timber-framed walls infilled with brick (known as nogging), and brick wall linings are frequently seen in Irish buildings of the eighteenth and nineteenth centuries. In nearly all cases, this brickwork was plastered over and never intended to be seen. The stripping of plasterwork to expose internal brickwork is generally unsatisfactory because of the inferior quality of the brick selected for that specific purpose, the condition and appearance of the mortar joints and a frequently lower standard of overall workmanship. Sometimes however, brick vaults in basements and internal brickwork in garden buildings, stables, and out buildings were intended to be seen and were not rendered but simply lime-washed. This is an attractive finish that is practical and easy to maintain. Wherever possible, limewash finishes should be maintained or renewed.

Handmade brick used in a brick nogged internal partition, now exposed where the original plaster coating has fallen away

BRICK AND STONE FAÇADES

The combined use of brick walling with stone dressings articulating building façades is an ancient practice and widespread in many historic buildings in Ireland. A particular problem can arise where brickwork is combined with limestone in façades.

Some brickwork is liable to deteriorate because in polluted atmospheres, the sulphur contained within acid rain attacks the calcium carbonate and creates calcium sulphate which, if the building is not properly detailed, may wash down from the limestone onto the brickwork below. This downwash is absorbed into the bricks and expands with crystallisation causing the brick faces to spall.

The decorative brick and stone façade of the former Kildare Street Club, Dublin designed by Deane and Woodward and built in 1859-61

GARDEN WALLS

Brick was considered to be a handsome material for garden walls and a most convenient surface onto which to nail trellises and plant supports. It also had beneficial properties as a heat-retaining material with insulating benefits that aided plant propagation. The widespread use of brick for this purpose suggests that the material was produced locally. Garden structures can often be the only fragments surviving from former demesnes and, as such, can yield important archaeological information about early building materials and methods of construction.

Eighteenth-century garden walls at Festina Lente, Bray, Co. Wicklow

Rusticated brickwork at Ballyannan, Co. Cork. The detailed view shows beautiful axed work

BRICK PAVING

Bricks, of appropriate hardness and durability, have a long history of use for internal flooring, external paving, and roads. Floor paving with brick is not uncommon in eighteenth-century cellars, outhouses, and washhouses.

Decorative brickwork

The term 'decorative brickwork' covers a range of non-standard brickwork, deliberately detailed to display colour, light and shade, or textural contrast of all, or specific parts of, a façade. It was often combined with raised or recessed configuration of the brickwork through the skilful use of plain or specifically-shaped bricks called 'specials'.

Seventeenth and eighteenth-century examples of decorative brickwork consist of cut-moulded (cut-and-rubbed to shape) or purpose-moulded (cast to the required shape) brick. These special brick shapes are to be seen in brick plinths, plat bands, cornices, dentil and string courses, and surrounds to openings. Evidence of the early use of decorative brickwork can be gleaned from a study of Jigginstown House where there is use of cut-and-rubbed features of a buff coloured brick in

contrast to the general red brick creating polychromatic brickwork. There is one surviving example of an unusual deep undulating cut-and-rubbed window arch of red and buff coloured bricks. The delightful brick-built pavilion in the grounds of Ballyannan Castle (c.1660), near Midleton, County Cork, has cut and rubbed projecting rustication and two niches set either side of the arched main entrance. The bricks were deliberately finished with strokes of a brick axe.

The Royal Hospital, Kilmainham, Dublin, and Beaulieu House, County Louth, both feature decorative cornices, string courses, and window surrounds in brick although, in the case of the Royal Hospital, this work is concealed by a later rendering of the façades. Old Clonmannon House (early eighteenth century), County Wicklow, displays very unusual rustication and modelling of the façade in the style of the architect Inigo Jones whilst Shannongrove (1709), County Limerick, has unusual panelled brick chimneys with raised brick decoration in the panels.

The use of bricks in the Georgian period tended to be more subdued, in line with the more sober Palladian and Neoclassical styles of architecture then prevailing. Brick buildings constructed at this time tend to have plain, flat façades of fine handmade bricks.

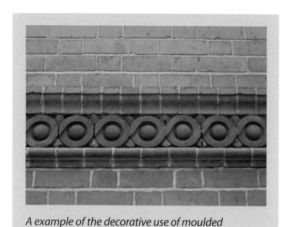

A example of the decorative use of moulded brickwork and terracotta in a stringcourse

Nineteenth century machine-made brick became so sophisticated that it was possible to manufacture bricks in a huge variety of ornamental shapes, and in a range of bright colours, suitable for decorative use on elaborate mouldings, friezes, panels, arch mouldings, window aprons, scrolls, plinths and ventilation bricks.

In the twentieth century, new construction methods allowed greater opportunities for brick to be used decoratively. The public housing blocks of the 1930s in Dublin, for example, demonstrate that the architect, Herbert Simms (1898-1948), had a particular interest in brick, using it decoratively in forms such as stack bond, basket weave, and herring bone patterns. Internationally, Modernist architects, such as Frank Lloyd Wright and Alvar Aalto, had bricks produced for their buildings that were longer and thinner than the standard brick proportions. In Ireland, Michael Scott selected a non-standard slim brick for the base of Busáras (1953) in Dublin.

The Arts and Crafts Movement in the late nineteenth century promoted the use of handcrafted building materials, including handmade bricks, as in this example of a house at Talbot's Inch village, Co. Kilkenny designed by the architect William A. Scott and built 1896-1904

Recently there has been a renewed interest in replicating traditional brick bonding patterns in modern Irish buildings, although these are executed in modern single skin facing brickwork. Patterns such as Monk bond, Stack bond, Flemish bond and Flemish garden wall bond have been used to good effect in contemporary buildings providing more lively patterns than the monotonous stretcher bond of standard half-brick walling.

Polychromatic brickwork

Although the use of multi-coloured brick for decorative patterning has a long history in England and continental Europe, most polychromatic brickwork in Ireland dates from the nineteenth century as imported coloured bricks became more widely available. However, Jigginstown House provides an early example of different coloured bricks, reds and buffs, used decoratively. In the twentieth century there was a minor fashion, particularly in the 1940s and 50s, to use over-burnt and misshapen bricks for decorative purposes in façades.

Polychromatic brickwork at the Mageogh Home, Rathmines, Dublin dating from 1878

Terracotta and faïence

The description 'terracotta' (literally meaning 'baked earth') is used to describe a ceramic material that is finer-grained than brick. It is one of the oldest building materials known to man but in this country its use is primarily associated with the Gothic Revival in the nineteenth century when it provided a cheap, yet attractive, replacement for stone, combining durability with low maintenance. It is made from freshly quarried, finely ground clay mixed with grog (a powder ground from previously-fired clay) and was moulded to form chimney pots and decorative architectural features. It was also used in the form of large hollow moulded blocks which could be filled with concrete if required, set with mortar joints, and anchored with metal cramps back to the main wall of a building for cornices, string courses, or other functional and/or decorative features.

Faïence is terracotta which has been re-fired and, as a building material, was used in large flat ceramic slabs, or tiles, set on a mortar bed to form an ashlar facing to a building. Much of the terracotta and faïence found in Irish buildings was imported from English or Welsh manufacturers, although some of the larger brickmaking companies in Ireland manufactured terracotta towards the end of the nineteenth century when it was at the height of its popularity as a building material.

Both materials were made in a variety of natural colours ranging between buff and red. Glazing was used to provide extra protection and a wider variety of colours. The material is of similar quality to that used for tiles or pottery, and is fired to a temperature in excess of 1000°C to achieve a high degree of vitrification. Terracotta and faïence possess properties that make them resistant to pollution. They can be fired with a hardness, compactness and sharpness of detail not normally obtainable with brick and can be cast in large sizes with hollowed out areas that aid drying, and firing, and reduce weight. These cavities must be filled with a lime or cement concrete before the material is laid.

Stoneware products

Stoneware is a term used to describe a highly vitrified ceramic that looks superficially like stone. Its unique appearance derives from its composition of kaolinitic clay and other minerals. Coade Stone, and other stoneware products such as those made by Van Spangen & Powell of London, are essentially forms of terracotta made from patented recipes. Coade Stone is made of a proprietary off-white vitreous material, cast in moulds and fired at high temperatures. From 1767 until around 1840, the Coade factory (initially at Lyme Regis, but later Lambeth, London) under Eleanor Coade and her daughter, supplied architectural ornamentation to builders and architects all over Britain and Ireland, and further afield. The Coade Stone factory produced sculpted figures, column cappings, plaques, medallions, fountains and garden furniture. There are many surviving examples of Coade Stone features in Ireland. The ceramic body is quite durable but, as with terracotta, it can be damaged by the expansive action of the rusting of iron fixings.

Burton's, Dame St, Dublin, designed in 1929 by Harry Wilson, is an example of high quality faïence cladding used to form a giant classical order to the façade

This terracotta panel has been carefully repaired following the removal on an automatic teller machine which had been inserted beneath the window

3. Identifying Problems in Brickwork

The most common problems likely to be encountered by owners of brick buildings are the decay of the joints in the brickwork and/or the decay of individual bricks in specific areas and in varying amounts. The causes of such decay will vary. They may be related to particular structural problems or failures, or may be simply the normal effects of weathering from rain and frost. Water in its different forms is the main agent of decay and brickwork, like all other building materials, needs to be correctly detailed to minimise the impact of driving rain and to cut down the potential for water saturation. Maintenance of rainwater goods, flashings and drainage are also essential to prevent damage.

Inspection and survey

Historic brickwork will deteriorate and decay if not properly maintained or if it is subjected to inappropriate repair works. Decay can be caused by a number of factors, most of which are the result of water penetration and the saturation of the brickwork.

The main signs that something is wrong with brickwork are:

> cracks or bulges

> bricks becoming loosened or dislodged

> spalling (deterioration of the surface of bricks)

> surface staining from organic growth

> efflorescence (white powdery residue on bricks)

> algae growth

> soft, loose or crumbling mortar

Where these symptoms are noticed, action should be taken to establish the cause of the defect and to put it right. Areas of risk are the higher and more exposed parts of a building such as chimneystacks and parapet walls. It is important to examine these more inaccessible parts of the building in any inspection. Alternatively, isolated patches of brickwork may become saturated due to leaking gutters or downpipes, damaged internal water pipes or slipped flashings.

Regular inspection and maintenance of building fabric are at the heart of good conservation practice. Maintenance is routine work necessary to keep the fabric of the building in good repair. Typically, for a brick-faced structure, this will require periodic inspection and checking of gutters and rainwater goods to ensure that the masonry is not receiving excessive amounts of water and taking particular note of the condition of the more exposed parts of the building, such as the parapet walls and chimneys. For further advice on maintenance refer to the Advice Series booklet – *Maintenance, a Guide to the Care of Older Buildings.*

Repair works are those beyond the scope of regular maintenance. Repair will be required to remedy significant decay or damage caused by neglect, weathering, or wear-and-tear over time. The object of a successful repair is to return the building to good order without alteration or restoration. Building inspection should identify defects and prioritise repairs under the headings of 'urgent', 'short-term', 'medium-term', and 'long-term' works.

To determine the true causes of failure and arrive at the best methods of repair, accurate information will be needed on the element of brickwork to be repaired. It will be necessary to understand the building's history, form, structure, materials, and original craft methods. For brickwork this should typically include information about:

> wall construction

> type, age, colour, texture and size of the brick

> type(s) of brick bonding used

> style(s) of joint finish

> orientation of façade

> detailing at openings – heads, reveals, sills

> decorative features such as the use of purpose-made or cut-moulded bricks, or use of clay creasing tiles

> materials used for mortars

> condition of the brickwork joints

> any particular surface treatments

> weathering details and how they are performing

> previous interventions and repairs

> signs of movement such as distress-cracking or bulging and whether this movement is active or inactive

> brickwork discolouration due to staining, salt attack, lime leaching, efflorescence

> signs of biological growth and invasive vegetation

Identifying structural problems

The most common sign of a structural fault in brickwork is **cracking**. This can be caused by structural movement, subsidence, unstable foundations, the effect of tree roots or defects in the original construction. Cracks can be minor and superficial, restricted to a few isolated bricks. However, extensive cracking is usually indicative of a serious problem and a structural appraisal by a suitably qualified structural engineer, experienced in dealing with traditionally-constructed masonry, is essential.

Façade brickwork showing evidence of structural movement in the cracks stretching between the windows

Common structural defects in brickwork can be caused by a number of different reasons, such as cracking due to settlement or problems with rainwater goods. The defects may also be the result of the original use of inferior materials, bad original detailing, or poor craft practices, such as improper bonding. In the Georgian period, for example, the prolific use of 'snapped' headers in façades mean that, while the outer skin of brickwork looks like a typical 9-inch (225mm) solid wall of bonded brickwork, it is in reality only a half-brick-thick veneer, infrequently tied-in to the backing brickwork. As with most historic buildings, the Georgians graded their bricks from the clamp or

kiln. The best quality bricks and mortar were used where appearance mattered, and their inferior counterparts were used where the brickwork was to be concealed. This led to a situation where the load-bearing brickwork was often made with the poorest quality bricks while the facing bricks, which carried little or none of the structural load, were of the highest quality. Party walls between dwellings in terraces were often infrequently tied-in to external walls so that there was no effective restraint between floor levels. Differential behaviour of under-fired bricks laid in weak mortar can lead to bulging of the wall.

Furthermore, the inner brickwork of the wall is often found to contain **built-in bonding timbers**. These bonding timbers were inserted into brick walls at intervals during construction as a temporary restraint in long walls being built at speed. These timbers were usually of softwood and can shrink, causing localised cracking. Timber was also commonly used to form lintels above door and window openings. The timber used for lintels tended to be of a higher quality and is less likely to cause such problems. Bonding timbers are also vulnerable in a damp external wall to attack from fungi and insects causing the timbers to deform or, in severe cases, collapse. When deformation of inner brickwork occurs to a significant extent, it can lead to a shearing of the bonding headers that connect the facing brickwork with the main wall behind and may cause the outer skin to collapse.

Bricks can be damaged by impact, in this case from a vehicle striking a brick archway

BULGES IN BRICKWORK

There is a range of reasons why bulges may occur in brick walls, the following is a list of some of the more typical causes:

> poor original workmanship and defects such as inadequate cross bonding (can be identified when the outer wall face is bulging and the inner wall face remains straight)

> decay of the structure in a variety of ways due to water penetration, e.g. leading to delamination of the wall

> rotting bonding timbers

> problems with changing ground conditions

> changes in loading on the wall

> previous inappropriate interventions, such as the enlargement of openings and the formation of new openings in a wall without sufficient support

Bulging of a brick wall may be of minor or more serious concern. Often, the minor movements which occur throughout the life of structures lead to gentle bowing which is part of the historic character and charm of the structure and, in such cases where there is no concern regarding structural integrity, then the principle of minimum intervention should be observed. However, where bulging is found it is recommended to seek the advice of a structural engineer with a knowledge and experience of traditional buildings – choosing the right engineer can often result in less radical, more sensitive and often cheaper solutions.

Rear extensions, returns, and **bay windows,** often built with slender and poorly-bonded piers between openings, were commonly erected after the main construction of the building was complete. They were often built upon shallower foundations, and consequently the tying-in between later and earlier brickwork can be compromised and cracks may appear at the junction.

In **chimney construction**, the practice of using lime mortar to line or parge the inner face of flues can conceal poor bonding of the masonry separating individual flues on multi-flued chimneys. Expansion and contraction as a result of years of intermittent heating and cooling cycles, as well as the aggressive chemical action of condensing hot gases, leave soluble sulphates that attack and remove these flue linings, exposing the bonding problems.

Dealing with structural defects

When structural defects are identified, it is strongly recommended that the advice of a structural engineer with a knowledge and experience of older buildings is sought. In all instances the causes of failure should first be correctly diagnosed in order to plan the appropriate repair works.

REPAIRING CRACKS

Minor cracks can be repaired by carefully cutting out the affected areas of brick, replacing fractured bricks, and repointing using a mortar appropriate to the existing brickwork. Where major cracking has occurred, or where bricks are displaced or out of alignment due to structural movement, specific repair works will need to be planned and directed by a structural engineer experienced in the repair of traditional structures.

DEALING WITH BULGING IN A BRICK WALL

Each situation will require a specific solution and it should always be the primary aim to repair the brickwork in situ, rather than take down and rebuild. However, there are occasions when the structural defect is such that the appropriate solution will be to carefully take down the damaged section and rebuild it using the original bricks. In such cases, the section to be taken down should firstly be recorded and then carefully dismantled in such a way as to maximise the retention of whole bricks for reuse. When rebuilding, matching historic bonding patterns and pointing materials and techniques should be used. This is specialised work and will require to be designed, specified and overseen on site by a suitably-qualified structural engineer. The conservation officer in the local authority should be consulted before any works are undertaken.

There is also a range of repair techniques available depending on the specific problem, the severity of it, location of bulge, and the like. The primary repair solution involves tying the bulging wall to a sound structural element and there are several different approaches to tying. Sometimes, where an external wall is being tied back to the structure, the tie will be fixed to the wall with an anchor plate. These are commonly found on historic buildings, but it is also sometimes possible to conceal the fixing. It is important that the repair solution does not result in making a structure overly rigid that was designed to have flexibility. This can create stresses in the building which may induce new and more serious problems whether in the brickwork or elsewhere.

Sometimes the deformation of a wall is such that tying back will not be sufficient and the wall, or part of it, may need to be taken down and rebuilt. Generally, if a defect is left unattended for a long period, the likelihood of such radical solutions being required becomes greater. The earlier a problem is identified and repair is undertaken, the simpler, and generally cheaper, the solution will be. Always with such structural repairs the advice of a structural engineer experienced and expert in traditional building construction will be required.

REPAIR OF CHIMNEYSTACKS

The exposed parts of buildings, such as chimneystacks, are particularly vulnerable to the effects of severe weathering and structural failure.

The chimneys found in old buildings are usually unlined, tall and heavy in construction, and now often redundant. They may present different problems to chimneys in modern buildings including leaning, fractured or loose brickwork caused by movement, excessive water ingress contributing to frost and sulphate attack, plant growth, failure of protective mortar cappings, flaunching and fillets and the loss of mortar parging to the inner faces of flues.

Erosion of both bricks and mortar joints by the action of wind, rain (and accompanying frost and sulphate attack) can seriously weaken a chimneystack. If the brickwork of the chimney is quarter-bonded, one-brick-thick, reasonably plumb and otherwise structurally sound, there will usually be enough support for individual badly-eroded bricks to be carefully cut out and replaced and the joints repointed. This may not be possible with a chimney stack of a single, half-brick width laid in stretcher bond.

In some instances, a chimneystack may be so out of plumb, extensively fractured, and with eroding mortar and loosened masonry that it presents a public safety issue. It also has the potential to damage other parts of the building should it collapse. In such circumstances careful recording, disassembly, and accurate reconstruction may be the only practical solution.

Because of their high exposure, chimneystacks are vulnerable to decay and defects in stacks may be difficult to spot because of their relative inaccessibility. However, their condition should be carefully monitored to avoid any public safety issues arising

When chimney flues are redundant it is important not to fully close them. These flues may provide important ventilation to the interior of the building. Generally it is best to maintain ventilation in the flue and not to carry out any works that would prevent the chimney being reopened and brought back into use at a later time. Flues can be temporarily capped-off by means of proprietary ceramic ventilated flue terminals or by using a slate or lead capping, slotted to provide adequate ventilation.

Decorative terracotta chimney pots should always be retained and, where repair is necessary, this is best carried out in situ. If they are badly damaged and repair in situ is not possible, they should be recorded in their original position before being taken down for professional repair and later reinstatement.

REPAIR OF PARAPET WALLS

Damage to brickwork is most frequent where any part of a wall is exposed on both sides. Parapet walls are exposed to saturation and the extremes of weather. They do not benefit from radiant warmth from inside the building and are more vulnerable to frost damage and salt attack than brickwork lower down the façade.

Spalled bricks should be carefully cut out, and either reversed or replaced. Replacement bricks should be matching reclaimed or new bricks, set with full joints in a specified mortar of an appropriate class of hydraulic lime to suit the degree of exposure. Care should be taken to ensure that the mortar of the connecting cross-joints is not cracked or missing – otherwise rainwater may be allowed down into the parapet brickwork. Where the joints are damaged, they should be fully cut out and repointed with hydraulic lime mortar. Where a coping stone has failed it should be carefully removed and re-laid using all original units where possible, or matching replacements where not. It is considered good practice to take the opportunity to introduce a damp proof course (dpc) below the coping, even if this was not part of the original construction. The dpc should be positioned either directly below the coping or, if it would interfere with the bond to the brickwork, on the penultimate course of bricks below.

The gutters behind parapet walls are difficult to access and therefore are often poorly maintained. Many parapet walls show evidence of having been reconstructed over the lifetime of the building. This illustration shows the use of inappropriate replacement bricks in the repair of the wall

If parapet brickwork has failed it should be carefully recorded and taken down. All bricks capable of re-use should be scraped clean of old mortar and stored in dry conditions until rebuilding is ready to begin. The brickwork should then be reconstructed to follow the original in level, line, height and bonding pattern. Such cases offer an opportunity to either fully restore or replace all the leadwork of the parapet guttering and to fit a dpc above, as well as below, the coping.

The maintenance of all parapet walls should pay particular attention to the parapet gutter that collects and discharges rainwater into the hopper-head and/or downpipe. The parapet gutter should be provided, maintained, repaired, or replaced as required. It may sometimes be advisable to protect the highly porous inside face of a parapet with a specified hydraulic lime render, or a detail using slate or leadwork.

It is not uncommon in Ireland to find parapets, and upper sections of brick façades, that have been rebuilt in the past with bricks that do not match the original façade bricks, either in size, quality, or colour. Provided that the earlier repair works are structurally sound, they should be respected as they form part of the building's history. However, such repairs often cause an aesthetic dilemma for building owners, who may view them as being unsightly. If repointing of the particular façade is necessary, it may be possible to improve the overall appearance of the façade through techniques such as colour-washing. However, such works should be very carefully considered in the context of the building location. If the building forms part of a terrace, changes in its appearance may affect the entire group of buildings. Planning permission may be required.

Brickwork decay

WATER SATURATION

One of the most common causes of deterioration and failure of brickwork is water saturation. Water can percolate deep into masonry by capillary action. It can be a particular problem on exposed areas of a building, such as parapets and chimneystacks and in the vicinity of leaking rainwater pipes. Bricks differ in their tolerance of wet conditions according to their material properties.

Causes of excessive water penetration can include:

> rising damp

> rainwater ponding at the base of walls

> encroaching vegetation

> windblown rain

> failure of roof systems

> defective rainwater goods

> failed mortar joints to copings

> slipped or damaged flashings

Weathering of brickwork can in some cases be severe. In this case, the decay may have been exacerbated by the mortar being too strong

FROST DAMAGE

Different brick types will vary in their ability to withstand frost damage. Porous bricks will absorb more water and some may have poorer frost resistance than denser bricks. It should be noted, however, that there is no dependable correlation between strength or water absorption and frost resistance. Frost resistance relates to the pore structure of the brick. Frost damage results when the water absorbed by the brick expands on freezing, breaking the brick apart. Where this occurs it may be necessary to replace damaged bricks. It is also essential to discover and remedy the source of the water that has saturated the bricks and to make good such defects as leaking rainwater pipes or overflowing gutters.

SALT CRYSTALLISATION

In historic brickwork, soluble salts present in the adjacent sub-soil may be carried up a wall by rising damp. Salts may also be present in the bricks themselves. The saturation of brickwork can cause the movement of salts through the wall to the surface of the brick. If these salts crystallise within the body of the brick wall they cause 'sub-florescence'. Because the crystals of salt expand in size, this can result in the spalling of the faces of the bricks. The white powder caused by salts crystallising on the surface of the brick or mortar is known as 'efflorescence'. Efflorescence is normally harmless, though while it lasts it can be aesthetically disfiguring. Where it appears, it should be brushed off and collected as otherwise the salts will continue to attract moisture and prevent the brick surface from drying.

ATMOSPHERIC POLLUTION

Brickwork can be affected by chemical attack from atmospheric pollutants on surfaces that are not regularly washed clean by rain. These include areas directly under windowsills and projecting dressings where there is an accumulation of encrusted dirt. Where deposits remain on the surface of brick they can, in time, lead to the formation of destructive salts.

Soluble salts visible on the surface of this brickwork have been caused by rising damp in the wall. The moss growth present is another symptom of the excessive dampness of the bricks the cause of which needs to be diagnosed and treated

SULPHATE ATTACK

Historic brickwork on chimneystacks is subject to soluble sulphates in condensing gases. These areas are most susceptible to the harmful effect of sulphate attack. Sulphate attack can also occur with mortars based solely on Ordinary Portland Cement (which contain alite) when they come in contact with soluble sulphates, such as those that occur in the groundwater of clay soils. The resultant expansive action can be seen as a thin linear crack through the bed joints.

DAMAGE FROM VEGETATION

Unchecked vegetation can be harmful to brick structures. Ivy, in particular, can cause serious harm if allowed to grow on damaged surfaces and penetrate with its root system into the wall core. Other climbing plants, while not penetrating the wall with roots, should not be allowed to grow to the extent that they cover up or conceal defects in the brick wall behind, or hold moisture and prevent the wall from drying out naturally. Moss growing on brickwork is a sure sign of a saturated wall and the growth will damage bricks further by encouraging more water retention against the face of the brickwork.

Some safety issues

GETTING READY

Wear the right clothes when carrying out maintenance inspections. Wear shoes, or boots, with a good grip. Do not wear clothes with trailing pieces or cords as these may catch and cause you to fall. Heavy-duty gloves, safety goggles, and masks are recommended for clearing gutters and when clearing up bird droppings because of the associated health risks.

WORKING AT A HEIGHT

Carrying out maintenance inspections at a height is hazardous. If you do not feel safe, or are nervous working at a height, then get professional help with the work.

Using ladders is a major safety issue. Avoid working on roofs or on ladders in windy, wet, or icy weather conditions. It is always safest not to work alone. You should have someone competent with you to hold the ladder. Take care of people below when working at a height to avoid injuries caused by falling or thrown objects. Always use a ladder that is in good condition and of the correct height. Make sure it is secure, angled correctly with the top resting against a solid surface (not a gutter or a fascia). When climbing ladders make sure you have both hands free. Always work so you can have one hand on the ladder at all times, have a good handhold, and do not overreach.

With many buildings that are larger or higher than an average dwelling, it may not be safe for an untrained person to carry out even the simplest maintenance or repair tasks. In fact, it is not advisable for any untrained person to work from ladders above one-storey high. If you have a building that is too tall for safe working from a ladder, you should consider installing a permanent, properly-designed means of access to roof level. Some works may require planning permission and you should consult your planning authority first. If it is not possible to provide a permanent means of access to a roof, you could consider hiring, or investing in, a properly-designed mobile scaffold tower or a mobile elevated working platform.

For further information on the safety issues of inspecting or working on roofs, see the Health & Safety Authority's publication: *Code of Practice for Safety in Roofwork*.

WORKING WITH LIME

Quicklime, delivered for slaking, is a highly hygroscopic material and hence its use with water can be very dangerous. Full eye protection and protective clothing, including gauntlet gloves, as well as barrier creams on exposed skin, are important. All cuts must be kept clean and covered. When not in use the quicklime should be stored in sealed containers and in a shed within an area deliberately set aside for such use. Only craftworkers skilled and experienced in such work should be permitted to handle quicklime and to undertake on-site slaking.

Slaked lime, as calcium hydroxide, delivered either as putty or dry-hydrate, is highly caustic. Long-term working without gloves, leading to its direct contact with the skin can cause the skin to dehydrate and even burn. It should be used with great care in accordance with all current safety regulations. Gloves and barrier creams are essential skin protection, as are goggles for the eyes. Like cement, dry-hydrated non-hydraulic, or hydraulic limes can be inhaled during mortar preparation, so this should always be undertaken outside and face masks worn; the same precautions should also be followed when using powdered pigments. Also, once dry-hydrated limes are mixed with water, like lime putty, avoidance of direct contact with the skin once again becomes critically important.

4. Repairing Brickwork

This section deals with the options available for the localised repair of damaged or decayed bricks and the mortar joints between them. Individual bricks can be repaired using a specialised technique of mortar or 'plastic' repair or can be reversed or replaced. The mortar in the joints between bricks plays an essential role in the overall performance of the brickwork and in the visual appearance of a wall. The use of inappropriate repair materials or repointing techniques is a common cause of problems with historic brickwork.

Repair techniques for bricks

REPLACING WHOLE BRICKS

Large-scale replacement of bricks in a historic façade should, wherever possible, be avoided. Individual bricks that have been damaged or decayed to the extent that their structural integrity is in doubt may require replacement. Where this is necessary, the bricks should be accurately identified, and the specific type of repairs recorded on marked-up drawings.

Where original bricks cannot be utilised, it will be necessary to source replacement bricks. These should always match the originals in size, colour, texture, porosity, and durability. It may be necessary to have them specially manufactured for the job. There are traditional brickmakers who manufacture handmade or machine-made bricks to specification for remedial work. The work of cutting-out defective bricks requires an experienced contractor. Replacement should include brushing all voids clean of debris, dampening, and placing the brick onto, and surrounded by, a full bed of lime mortar.

Reclaimed or salvaged bricks should always be carefully inspected to ensure that they are deemed fit for replacement purposes, particularly with regard to external weathering. Most companies selling salvaged building materials accept no liability for faults and weaknesses in them. Unlike new materials, salvaged bricks do not have to meet test regulations as to their performance. A pallet of bricks supplied by a reclamation company may contain bricks of different grades, types and qualities, and some may be unsuited to being placed in the weather and surviving exposure. Placed in an external location today, such bricks would quickly deteriorate.

Bricks that were originally set in a lime-based mortar can be readily cleaned off and reused in repairs but it is important to establish the provenance of any reclaimed bricks to ensure that they have not been taken from another historic building that should not have been demolished in the first place

It is always important to determine the provenance of salvaged building materials to ensure that the bricks have come from a traceable source, have not resulted from the unauthorised destruction of another historic building and were originally used in an external location. In some rare cases, it may be possible to source replacement bricks from elsewhere in the historic building or from contemporary structures within its grounds. For example, there may be derelict outbuildings or garden walls that were built of the same brick or bricks may have been salvaged from previous authorised alterations to the building. Taking such bricks from their original location will require expert assessment and advice on all the implications.

Replacement bricks may at first appear bright in comparison with the surrounding original brickwork. Providing care has been taken in selecting appropriate replacement bricks, they will tone down naturally under the influence of weathering and atmospheric pollution. However, sometimes it will be desirable to accelerate this process and tone down the appearance of the new bricks immediately so that they blend in. Techniques such as applying a dilute colour wash or soot should only be undertaken after samples have been carried out on unobtrusive parts of the façade, and an assessment made of the effects of the treatment.

REVERSING BRICKS

For certain repair works it may be an option to reverse individual decayed or damaged bricks. In this process, a damaged brick is carefully cut out and turned through 180° and re-laid into its original position. The effectiveness of this repair technique depends on the soundness of the overall brick. There is little point in reversing a brick if the new face will deteriorate in the same way as the original face once exposed to the weather. Bricks with minor defects may not warrant being cut out and reversed and, providing there is no damp ingress or structural concerns, can be left alone. Reversing bricks requires skill and can be a time-consuming task. There may also be difficulties in successfully cleaning mortar off the new face of the brick.

MORTAR OR 'PLASTIC' REPAIR

Methods for repairing localised damage of individual bricks can include filling small holes or repairing minor damage to otherwise sound bricks using a lime mortar mix, coloured to match the brick. This is a specialised technique called mortar repair or sometimes 'plastic repair'. It should only be used as a temporary repair solution until such time as the correct remedial work can be carried out. It should only be used in localised repairs. Large areas should never be repaired using plastic repairs. It can be time-consuming work and requires a skilled craftsperson, but, provided that structural requirements are met, it is preferable to replacing whole historic bricks. Good repair work will require thorough preparation of the cavities to be filled, followed by careful filling in individual well-compacted layers. For this reason, mortar repair has often being compared with dental work in filling cavities in teeth. Mortar repair is a useful technique

Remedial work in the form of a quality pigmented mortar repair. It shows that, when necessary, and executed with great skill, a mortar repair can provide a temporary repair that achieves the desired effect

where there is minor and isolated decay of brick, but it is not recommended where there is deterioration of brickwork on a large scale.

Proprietary brick repair mortars should be viewed with caution. They can be cementitious and cause problems to historic brickwork in the longer term.

BRICK SLIPS

Brick repair using brick slips (thin tiles of brick) is only used in very limited situations when it is not possible to remove the whole brick without causing greater damage. This repair method is also mainly used for individual brick repairs and is not recommended for large sections of repair. The brick slips should match the existing brick and be a minimum of 25mm (and preferably 50mm) thick, applied to the clean, even and pre-wetted surface with a bed of lime mortar to finish flush with the adjacent brickwork to avoid loosing historic detail and profile. Brick slip repairs should not be used on exposed locations such as parapets and chimney stacks. Thinner, proprietary brick slips which are intended for use in modern construction (and frequently seen on brickmakers' sample boards) and are applied with epoxy resins should never be used in historic building repair.

Repair of mortars and pointing

The deterioration of mortars is one of the most common problems that arises in brickwork façades. A traditional mortar is made of three principal components: a binder (typically, but after the mid-nineteenth century not exclusively, lime), an aggregate (or sand), and water. A mortar can fail because of the poor quality of, or the use of the wrong type of, original binder or aggregate. The ratio of aggregate and binder can also be at fault, as can poor preparation and application.

Joints will weather-out for a variety of reasons, such as the degree of exposure, failed flashings, or leaking rainwater goods. Eventually the decision to repoint or partially repoint has to be considered, especially if failed mortar is allowing moisture to penetrate the wall. As a rule-of-thumb, if a joint has eroded back as deep as it is wide, repointing should be considered. Earlier ill-advised repairs, or repointing, are major causes of failure of historic brickwork. This is particularly the case where the earlier repointing was carried out using a hard cement-based mortar on soft handmade bricks bedded in a lime-based mortar.

Occasionally the decision may have to be made to leave cement repointing untouched, if careful and controlled trials to determine the best method of cutting-out reveal that its removal would result in unacceptable damage to the vulnerable arrises of the brick.

Ill-advised repointing using cementitious mortar is seen on the brickwork to the right. It is not only visually unacceptable (using inappropriate heavy-handed weather struck and cut profile which is incorrect for the period of construction of the building) but will cause serious problems to the building in the long-term and will be impossible to remove without damage to the bricks

Soft, handmade bricks, such as these with a granulated structure, are particularly vulnerable to damage and decay as a result of poor-quality re-pointing

ANALYSING THE EXISTING MORTAR

Most historic structures were built using traditional lime-based mortar. The mortar joint system acts as a flexible gasket in thick-walled construction and is the conduit through which the masonry is able to breathe and accommodate normal thermal movement. If a building is to be repaired or repointed, the replacement mortar must match the original as closely as possible. Finding the correct type and ratio of the materials to be used will be crucial to the long-term welfare of the building.

The materials found in original bedding and pointing mortars offer important information. To determine the best replacement mortar for a particular building, the first step should be to undertake an analysis of the existing mortar. This, when carried out by experienced professionals, is a straightforward process. Mortar analysis typically comprises in situ visual appraisal – very dependent on the knowledge and experience of the individual involved – and a laboratory examination that seeks to determine the class of binder, aggregate type, size, and grading, and the ratio of binder to aggregate. Only full, uncrushed, sections of mortar – about 150mm long x 100mm wide – should be sent for laboratory analysis. Those who do laboratory sampling can also advise on suitable replacement mixes and several reputable companies now offer this service.

DESIGNING A REPLACEMENT MORTAR

There is no such thing as a standard recipe for a replacement lime mortar. Each historic building is different and will require its own individual assessment. The use of pre-mixed lime mortars should be avoided when working with historic brickwork. There were, and still remain, different classes of building limes and types and grades of aggregates, and all mortars must be specified to suit their particular situation. Mortar mixes are traditionally batched by volume (rather than by weight), so the type and grade of aggregate is fundamental in determining the proportion of binder needed for a quality, workable mix of sufficient strength and durability. Lime to sand ratios are often described as 1:3, but under analysis the majority of historic mortars are actually more lime-rich, with ratios typically varying between $1:1\frac{1}{2}$ and $1:2\frac{1}{2}$.

It is important that the contractor undertakes to make sample panels on site, to allow an assessment of the aesthetics of the mortar and profile. Samples should be executed on the same elevation as the wall to be repointed so they can be judged in the same light, and before the original joints are raked out. They should be given adequate time to cure and dry before decisions are taken. Samples are also a test of the skill of the operatives on site and establish an acceptable, specified standard of workmanship that can be referred back to during the course of works.

Existing mortar joints should not be cut out using mechanical cutters such as angle grinders as this will inevitably lead to damage of the edges, or arrises, of the bricks. The use of mechanical tools to remove cement repointing should generally never be used on historic brickwork unless specifically manufactured for use in historic brick repair and used only by experienced specialist conservators

MATCHING TRADITIONAL LIME MORTARS

New mortars for repairing, rebuilding, or repointing should match the original mortar (unless it was always defective) in the class of lime, aggregate type, ratio, colour, texture, and detailing. The new mortar should always be softer, in terms of compressive strength, and more porous than the brick masonry.

The colour of the aggregates, especially the choice of sands, is important because this is what gives the mortar its overall tone. The modern construction industry in Ireland tends to use aggregates made of crushed stone, whereas historic mortar almost always used pit-dug ('as-raised') alluvial sands. This can make it difficult to match the texture, colour, and performance of the original mortar. The grading of sand particles is very important because it affects the performance of the mortar, controls shrinkage, and contributes to the finished texture and strength of the mortar in its hardened state. With historic brickwork, the final colour and texture of the joint is particularly important. Depending on the bonding pattern used, the joints can form as much as 20% to 30% of the wall surface. Every effort should be made to source sands that provide the right colour balance, without the need for pigments.

TYPES OF BUILDING LIMES

The lime-based binders used in mortars for traditional thick-walled brickwork were historically of two types of lime (calcium carbonate):

1. The 95%+ pure, high calcium, 'air limes'. These harden slowly in contact with the atmosphere by absorbing carbon dioxide, or carbonating. The term 'air limes' was later changed to 'non-hydraulic limes' meaning that such a lime is incapable of hardening underwater, cut-off from the presence of the atmosphere.

2. 'Water limes', later termed 'hydraulic limes'. The sources of calcium carbonate used contain silica and alumina, which reacts with the lime to create a chemical set. They are able to set underwater, and/or to harden in the atmosphere by long term carbonation.

Hydraulic building limes were broadly divided into three classes of ascending strengths, accompanied by descending workability and porosity:

> Feebly hydraulic

> Moderately hydraulic

> Eminently hydraulic

Today modern building lime mortars fall within the following descriptions:

1. Non-hydraulic, pure lime mortars. These are usually based on the lime binder having been prepared ('slaked') to putty, or slaked to a powdered dry-hydrate and sold as 'High Calcium Lime'.

2. Artificial hydraulic mortars. These are often based on a mature non-hydraulic lime putty binder which, at the moment of use, is mixed with certain approved types of pozzolanic materials to create the setting characteristics required.

3. Hydraulic mortars. These are normally prepared from a powdered dry-hydrate, although the weakest class can be slaked to putty. It is classified in several grades, relating to ascending measures of compressive strength, by the approved Natural Hydraulic Lime (NHL) designation.

Hydraulic limes have always been preferred for external and structural works because of their all-important ability to set chemically – even in persistently damp environments – as well as providing better resistance to frost and harsh weather. Non-hydraulic limes are usually preferred for internal work, particularly for all types of plasters. Where only a non-hydraulic lime was locally available, the lack of strength was compensated for by simply increasing the ratio of lime in the mortar and the thickness, or mass, of the overall masonry. Modern non-hydraulic limes are purer than their historic equivalents and achieve much lower strengths. This should be taken into account when considering their use in historic brickwork.

WORKING WITH LIME MORTARS

The period from March to October was traditionally the time of year for building with lime mortars to protect them from frost damage before they had sufficiently cured and hardened. Today, with year-round contracting, if such work has to be carried out during the winter months it is essential that a fully-enclosed 'micro-enclosure' is created to maintain a minimum ambient temperature of 5°C, as well as provide protection from inclement weather.

REPOINTING HISTORIC BRICKWORK

Repointing historic brickwork should only be undertaken if absolutely necessary for the long-term welfare of the building. The work should be executed only by a bricklayer with proven experience of high quality work using traditional materials and craft techniques. Many buildings have significant areas of original joint finishes, or later good quality repointing that is still performing satisfactorily. In line with good conservation practice, this should be retained where possible.

Sound pointing should be left undisturbed, even if it has weathered back behind the wall face. Some weathering back of the historic mortar is to be expected. If, however, the original bedding mortar is severely eroded, and/or is soft and crumbly in texture, permitting moisture to penetrate deeply into the wall, then repointing will be necessary.

The mortar has weathered back or been washed out of this brickwork to a severe extent and it is now in urgent need of repair and repointing

The original joint finish may be quite weathered, making it difficult to establish the original profile and finish of the joint. An examination of less-exposed parts of the building, or of adjoining buildings of similar style and age, may be helpful in this respect. The final decision about what to do should be primarily concerned with the long-term health of the building and retaining the authentic aesthetic character.

Before any decision is made to repoint, a detailed visual analysis of the wall should be made to determine the nature and properties of the brick, as well as the characteristics and constituents of the original mortar. The analysis should also consider the construction detail in terms of bonding, width of joints, original joint profiles, finishing treatments, and texture.

Patch repointing of localised areas of deterioration is sometimes possible, but this still requires careful planning and execution in order to prevent a serious disruption to the overall aesthetics of the façade, or, in the case of a building in a terrace, to adjoining buildings. It is possible that planning permission may be required in some cases and it is advisable to contact the conservation officer at an early stage. Through analysis and sampling, as described above, suitable trial mortars should be prepared to establish a sound aesthetic and structural match for the constituent properties of the original.

Decayed lime mortar, whenever possible, should be carefully cut out using the appropriate hand tools. Mechanical tools are generally not necessary to remove old lime mortar. They may occasionally be needed in order to remove a later inappropriate cement-based repair or repointing mortar, but only in the hands of experienced specialist craftspeople. Disc-cutters should not be used on historic brickwork as they are difficult to control, damaging brick arrises and making the joints wider. Hand tools are always preferable, but should be used by skilled operatives in a way that respects, and does not damage, the historic brickwork. It is important to agree in advance the depth of cutting-out that will take place – generally 2 ½ times the width of the joint – and to make sure that the joints are finished with a squared seating. After cutting out, all surfaces should be vacuumed clean of debris to avoid any run-off staining the brickwork when the joints are being dampened in preparation for repointing operations.

Tools for repointing must be appropriately sized traditional brick jointers, finger trowels, or proprietary 'pointing keys' for placing, compacting, and dressing the pointing mortar into the joint. Standard pointing trowels, despite their name, are not suitable for this class of work.

Many present-day bricklayers do not have the skills necessary to execute historical joint profiles and finishes. This requires not only a selection of the correct traditional tools, equipment, materials, and knowledge, but also a well-taught and developed subtlety of skill. When tendering for repair works to historic brickwork, make sure that candidates are aware of the level of skill and craftsmanship that will be required from them in carrying out the works.

CHOICE OF JOINT PROFILE FOR REPOINTING

Once the case has been made for some repointing of brickwork then a decision has to be made regarding the choice of joint profile to be used. Various factors will influence this decision such as:

> the extent of repointing to be undertaken, that is whether the full elevation or only a part is to be repointed

> the overall condition of the existing joint finish

> the skill of the craftsperson carrying out the repointing

> the extent of evidence of the original joint finish. Replicating, or reinstating the original pointing profile, where this can be determined, will usually ensure the most appropriate solution as it follows the original architectural intention. It is important to note where particular regional styles have been used. Their replication in the repointing may often save distinctive traditional craft skills and techniques which would otherwise be lost

> the need to avoid using a pointing profile that is inappropriate to the original construction date of the property or for which there is no historical precedent. For example, weather-struck and cut pointing was introduced during the nineteenth century and would therefore be inappropriate for use when repointing Georgian brickwork.

There will be a need to match the surrounding faces of the joints which, through the action of the weather, have lost most of the original profile and have been left with an exposed aggregate surface that is otherwise sound.

Preparation of a joint for repointing

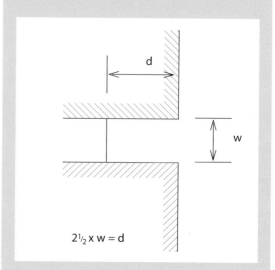

Step 1

Rake out mortar in joint to 2½ x width of joint. Brush out all loose material. Raking out to be done using manual tools to avoid damage to the brick arrises

Step 2

Pre-wet all surfaces of joint prior to applying mortar to desired profile (flush profile illustrated)

GAUGED BRICKWORK

Gauged brickwork was and remains a highly specialised craft that raised the practitioner to the status of a mason. The special soft-textured rubbing bricks, or rubbers, which are characteristic of this work are handcut and shaped to very precise dimensions and laid with narrow joints in a mortar of lime putty and fine silica sand.

Specialist advice should be sought on the causes of failure and appropriate methods of repair from an acknowledged authority. The repair of gauged brickwork requires the input of a highly-skilled, knowledgeable and experienced craftsperson. It is all too easy to destroy the beauty and accuracy of this type of brickwork by inappropriate materials and techniques.

Gauged brickwork of high quality was used in the brick architectural detailing of Beaulieu House, Co. Louth

Repairing terracotta and faïence

The durability of terracotta and faïence in their unglazed form relies on the hard thin skin formed in the firing process, called a 'fireskin'. The breakdown of this skin will lead to the deterioration and breakdown of the clay body core, which is not as durable. Crazing of the glaze or fireskin is common, but expanded crazing will eventually lead to ingress of moisture, which is often more of a problem with terracotta than with its fired clay cousin, brick. For this reason, cleaning terracotta and faïence is a very specialised process and these materials should never be cleaned with abrasive materials or chemicals.

Water-related problems are the most common cause of the failure of terracotta and faïence. Water that permeates a terracotta facing can cause rusting of the iron or steel anchoring system. Damage can range from staining or spalling of the surface to cracking and loosening of whole units, which may threaten the structural integrity of the entire building. Trapped water can lead to spalling, made worse when there is a glazed finish that may impede the drying-out process. This can lead to pressure, causing the glaze to blister or be forced off or, worse, some of the body of the element to break away. Rusting iron fixing, or anchoring, cramps can cause the same problem and are difficult to detect until the damage makes its presence known.

Serious problems within the units will not always be readily visible. Visual inspection will show only surface problems, such as crazing, spalling, and deterioration of mortar joints, but internal problems with anchoring, deterioration behind the surface and crumbling of the internal webbing will need to be investigated by endoscope and corrosion meter. This is a destructive investigation technique that requires drilling through the surface of the units. Documentation and recording is a vital component of this very specialised work.

The replacement of missing or badly damaged terracotta units should be made a high priority as they will permit water to enter the structure and may also increase the structural load on the remaining pieces. If replacement is necessary, whole units should be replaced, not parts, and plastic repairs are generally unsatisfactory. There are companies that can make replacement units (although not in Ireland). Some UK and Italian companies specialise in this area and can match clay body colours and glazes. Replacement units should be sized to take account of shrinkage in the manufacturing process. Careful recording and measuring is required, as drawings for replacement units need to be 12% larger than the finished item. Masonry construction skills are needed for replacing units. Materials should be replaced on a like-for-like basis. Alternative substitutes, such as concrete or glass-reinforced concrete (GRC) moulded units, behave and weather differently and should never be used for permanent replacement.

Grant aid

Conservation grants are available for the conservation and repair of protected structures and are administered by the planning authorities. You should contact the relevant one for guidance on whether the works you are planning are eligible for a grant and, if so, how to apply. These grants are not available for routine maintenance works, alterations, or improvements. The type of works must fit within the schedule of priorities set out by the planning authority. In order for works to qualify for these grants, they must be carried out in line with good conservation practice. Repair work following the guidance set out in this booklet should be considered as satisfying this requirement.

Other bodies also provide grants for building conservation projects. These include the Heritage Council and the Irish Georgian Society. Their contact details are included elsewhere in this guide.

Tax incentives are available under Section 482 of the Taxes Consolidation Act 1997 for expenditure incurred on the repair, maintenance, or restoration of certain buildings or gardens determined to be of significant horticultural, scientific, historical, architectural, or aesthetic interest. The building or garden must receive a determination from the Revenue Commissioners who must be satisfied that there is reasonable public access to the property. Application forms can be obtained from the Heritage Policy Unit, Department of the Environment, Heritage, and Local Government.

5. Cleaning Historic Brickwork

The decision on whether or not to clean historic brickwork can be a difficult one and should not be taken lightly. Unlike the cleaning of some types of stonework, the cleaning of brickwork is usually undertaken solely for aesthetic reasons. Before any decision is taken, careful research and a full assessment of the likely outcomes should be carried out. Signs of weathering and the patina of time are often part of the character and charm of historic brickwork, and cleaning will remove these. Over-aggressive cleaning methods may damage or remove the protective fireskin from the bricks. There are also times when weathered, dirty, and darkened surfaces are hiding defects or inappropriate repairs. In the latter case, unless work is carefully planned to correct these earlier mistakes, cleaning might not be a sensible approach.

On the other hand, there is the possibility that an accumulation of years of dirt, forming a hard crust on certain parts of the structure, may actually be detrimental to the historic fabric and in such cases careful removal is desirable. These residues can include sulphur dioxide deposits and skin formations resulting from the combustion of fossil fuels, ingrained grime, dirt, and soot.

Other surface deposits include:

> Chemical residues, oil, grease, and resins
> Exterior paint, graffiti, bitumen, and rubber
> Deposits related to fire-damage , formations, and residues
> Rust, verdigris, and other metallic formations
> Moss, lichens, algae, and other organic growths

In general, brickwork was intended to be bright. When mixed with other types of bricks, stone, or terracotta it was designed to achieve architectural effect by colour contrast. For this finish to be restored, careful cleaning may be desirable. In some instances, where repairs are proposed, cleaning will be necessary in advance so that it is possible to match properly the original colour of the brickwork with the correct repair materials. Advice should be sought from an acknowledged, independent specialist in this field, rather than a contractor, to determine the need for cleaning historic brickwork and to select the correct cleaning system.

It is essential to use only experienced contractors for this work and to have cleaning trials carried out before any decision is made about either the materials or methods to be used. Independent specialist advice should also be sought as techniques and cleaning methods are constantly being re-assessed and improved. What is appropriate for one type of brick may not suit another. Façades that contain a mixture of brick and stone, or Victorian façades of polychromatic brick, or brick combined with terracotta or faïence should be cleaned with great care as these materials differ in texture and hardness and will require different cleaning methods for each of their component parts. Careful examination of the condition of the brickwork is also vital in order to determine appropriate cleaning methods.

Brickwork stained with heavy sulphur dioxide deposits

To clean or not to clean

Deciding whether to clean brickwork or not involves careful investigation and consideration. Cleaning masonry is a highly specialised field and it may be neither necessary nor advisable for your building. In the past, the use of inappropriate cleaning techniques has resulted in considerable, and in some cases irreparable, damage to buildings. It is essential to seek independent objective professional advice from an acknowledged expert in historic masonry cleaning. Always check that the system the contractor is using is what has been specified and, where relevant, that the contractor is approved by the manufacturer of the system. Beware of taking advice from someone trying to sell you something, or from someone with a vested interest in increasing the scale and expense of work.

If the building is part of a terrace of brick buildings, consideration must be given to the overall effect of cleaning one of a group of buildings. Uncoordinated cleaning can create a patchwork effect and damage the architectural integrity of the group. In some cases, cleaning may require planning permission and the advice of the conservation officer in the local authority should be sought at an early stage.

Cleaning trials

A cleaning trial is essential. This trial will test the cleaning product and/or technique to determine the following:

> If the cleaning is practical and economically justified

> If the aesthetic results are desirable

> Which of the cleaning processes are successful and to eliminate those that are not

The cleaning trial should be specified, recorded, and supervised. It is vital to have quality 'before and after' photographs and all critical technical data should be accurately recorded. The trial should be undertaken on an area of brickwork truly representative of typical conditions, with enrichments and openings. The sample area to be cleaned should generally not be located on a prominent area of the building, nor should untried methods or materials be used on important features such as plaques or other decorative features until it has been determined that the chosen cleaning method is suitable and will not cause damage.

The cleaning trial is part of a detailed specification – this will encompass preparation, protection of property, materials, equipment, and techniques. It will also specify methods of work for operatives, surface repairs and treatments, and overall time costing.

Finally, only a contractor of proven experience of cleaning historic brickwork and fully trained in the system being specified, should be employed. In this respect it is always best to contact the company that owns the system, supplying all possible information on the proposed contractor, to confirm if they are on their list of approved specialist masonry cleaners.

Cleaning methods

The cleaning method chosen will depend on several different factors including the type and condition of the brickwork, and the type and extent of soiling. There are three basic cleaning methods for brickwork:

1. Cleaning with water

2. Chemical systems (including poulticing techniques)

3. Abrasive cleaning

CLEANING WITH WATER

This is the simplest way to clean down historic brickwork, including gauged work. Executed with care, cleaning with water need not damage the surface of soft, low-fired rubbing bricks. Clean, potable water is applied using fine, nebulous sprays to create a mist against the surface of the soiled masonry. Jets of water are unnecessary and should not be used as they can saturate the fabric and find entry points into the building. To be successful, and not cause damage to the building and its brickwork, it is essential that the minimum amount of water is used.

Soft, compact bristle brushes similar to nail or stencil brushes should be used. Even bristle brushes can scratch the surface of soft bricks. Ferrous metal brushes should not be used as small pieces of the iron bristles can break off and later rust, staining the brickwork. Most disfiguration and damage during washing, and the accompanying scouring by brushes, is as a result of the mobilisation of soluble salts, which appear as efflorescence on drying out.

Before washing historic masonry, all the points where water can penetrate must be temporarily sealed, and adequate drainage provided to cope with the run-off of the excess water. Sealing open joints can be achieved by the use of twists of waxed string or mastic beads. After cleaning, these are carefully stripped-out before repointing. On large façades, intermediate catchments for water run-off should be provided to avoid saturation of lower zones of brickwork.

Steam cleaning is currently gaining popularity for brickwork cleaning and can prove useful in removing algae, bitumen and modern paints and coatings. Proprietary systems are available that work at temperatures of 150ºC, killing the spores of biological growth and melting off paints and bitumen coatings.

Consideration should be given to avoiding any potential risks to health and safety of personnel and to avoiding damage to adjacent finishes such as painted joinery.

CHEMICAL WASHING

When dirt deposits are resistant to water cleaning, it may be acceptable to use mild detergents and other surfactants, with or without certain very dilute acids. Proprietary products containing hydrofluoric acid are highly corrosive and must always be used with extreme care, observing all of the manufacturer's health and safety advice. They are often much stronger than necessary and may be diluted with water several times below the recommended minimum. Only solutions with concentrations of below 1% should be used, with minimum periods of contact with the historic brickwork. Brick surfaces must be pre-wetted and after the cleaning material has been on the face of the brickwork (for typically 2 to 5 minutes) it must be very thoroughly washed off. Pre-wetting and washing off should be carried out with a pressure not exceeding 2760 kPa (400-psi).

Test, or trial, patches should always be approved and judged on their clean and fully dry appearance. Dangers associated with chemical systems include the formation of a white bloom on the bricks, resulting from too long a contact period with hydrofluoric acid, and damage caused by the careless use of the water lance. Glass, polished, and painted surfaces in the vicinity should be carefully protected from damage during cleaning, and operatives should have full face and hand/skin protection.

POULTICE CLEANING

Poulticing can be useful for treating specific types of heavy soiling or stains, especially complex forms such as oil, grease, or paint. Surfactants, or solvents, are placed against the face of the brickwork by means of a proprietary poultice following the manufacturers' instructions. The body of the poultice will usually be based on either clay or cellulose. After application it is normally covered with a thin plastic film to prevent it drying out. Poultice systems can make use of very dilute cleaning agents without the need to saturate or abrade the surface. They are normally removed by hand and by low-pressure water lance. In most cases it is advisable to approach a specialist to provide a purpose-made poultice to suit the individual cleaning requirements for maximum safety and economy.

Graffiti on historic brickwork should be cleaned off as soon as possible as it will become more difficult to remove if the paint is allowed to dry and harden. A suitable poultice may be the solution

This brickwork shows evidence of damage by over-heavy abrasive cleaning which has removed the fireskin from the bricks making them vulnerable to accelerated decay exacerbated by the cementitious pointing

ABRASIVE SYSTEMS

More brickwork has been damaged by the use of compressed air and abrasives, such as the sand or grit blasting methods, than by any other system. Abrasive materials blasted under pressure can destroy brickwork by removing the weathering surface of the brick. The use of sand blasting is now not permitted because of its health implications. Softer, finer, and rounder abrasives such as chalk or grape seed can be used successfully for cleaning brickwork in certain situations. It is possible, using small air abrasive tools and finer abrasives in the hands of a highly skilled and careful operative, to clean safely, but the hazards are great. In general abrasive cleaning systems should not used on historic brickwork.

There are other proprietary methods of mildly abrasive cleaning which work by developing a swirling vortex. In the hands of trained and experienced operatives, these systems very gently scour-off unwanted matter, such as carbon and lime based paints, without damaging the soft brick substrate. Such systems may be suitable for use on historic buildings in certain circumstances.

Renders and other surface treatments

REMOVAL OF RENDERS FROM HISTORIC BRICKWORK

Before stripping render or any other historic surface from a building, one should ask if it is really necessary. Removal may result in the loss of interesting earlier surfaces, or worse, can damage the historic substrate. In some cases it may not be possible to justify on historical or aesthetic grounds, particularly if the intention is to leave items stripped that were originally meant by the builders to be covered. Removing original render may expose masonry that was neither constructed as a weathering surface nor intended to be seen. It may also accelerate decay of the masonry and create pathways for the damaging ingress of moisture.

The removal of inappropriate, hard, and impervious cement-based renders from a brick façade, generally applied at much later date, can be desirable for the overall health of the building and also for aesthetic reasons, particularly if the building forms part of a brick-faced terrace. The decision to try to remove later renders, however, needs to be very carefully considered, and will generally require planning permission.

The surface of the brickwork may have been damaged in the process of preparation for applying a render, making successful removal impossible. It is essential to carry out extensive tests on different parts of the façade to determine the condition of the face of the brickwork, as well as its reaction to the action of removal, before any final decision is made. The set strength of the render and its grip to the substrate may result in it tearing away the all-important protective face, or fireskin, of the bricks beneath. It may destroy the original joint finish and create voids in the surface of the mortar. It may also be the case that the bricks beneath were deliberately scored, or scotched, to provide an improved key for that render. All of these problems are potentially serious and, if met, will be expensive, if not impossible, to remedy properly. If renders are being removed and replaced, it is strongly recommended that the underlying masonry is photographed or otherwise recorded while work is in progress.

SURFACE TREATMENTS

Properly detailed and laid brickwork does not require any surface coating to improve its weather resistance. The use of proprietary surface treatments such as water repellents should be avoided, including those marketed as being 'breathable' and those promoted as necessary to repel rainwater from the surface of external brickwork, to help keep brickwork clean, or as graffiti barriers. Many such surface treatments can cause irreversible damage to historic brickwork. The application of such coatings can actually encourage problems – they can reduce the evaporation of water from the masonry, trapping water and salts against or behind the wall surface where they can cause decay.

All proprietary coating materials will ultimately break down and this is unlikely to occur evenly across a brickwork façade. The result will be a patchy appearance and the possibility of the additional expense, and risk, of having to clean the brickwork to remove the remainder of the coating.

Historic buildings and the law

Under Part IV of the *Planning and Development Act 2000*, buildings that form part of the architectural heritage can be protected either by being designated a protected structure or by being located within an architectural conservation area.

Where a building is a protected structure (or has been proposed for protection) or is located within an architectural conservation area, the usual exemptions from requirements for planning permission do not apply. In the case of a protected structure any works, whether internal or external, which would materially affect its character will require planning permission. Legal protection also extends to other structures and features associated with a protected structure such as outbuildings, boundary walls, paving, railings and the like. In an architectural conservation area, any works to the exterior of a building which would affect the character of the area also require planning permission. Owners and occupiers of protected structures have a responsibility to maintain their buildings and not to damage them or allow them to fall into decay through neglect.

A notice was sent to every owner and occupier of a protected structure when the building first became protected but subsequent owners and occupiers will not have been notified. If you are not sure of the status of your building, check the Record of Protected Structures in the Development Plan for the area. If your building is a protected structure, or if it is located in an architectural conservation area, your planning authority will be able to tell you what this means for your particular property.

As an owner or occupier of a protected structure, you are entitled to ask the planning authority to issue a Declaration which will guide you in identifying works that would, or would not, require planning permission. Maintenance and repair works, if carried out in line with good conservation practice and the guidance contained within this booklet, will generally not require planning permission. More significant repairs, that would require the replacement of bricks, rebuilding areas of brickwork such as chimneys or parapets, or works that require significant re-pointing and/or cleaning of façade brickwork, will generally require planning permission. If you are in any doubt about particular proposed works, you should contact the conservation officer in your local authority for advice

For general advice on planning issues relating to architectural heritage, a publication entitled *Architectural Heritage Protection - guidelines for planning authorities* (2004) is available from the Government Publications Sales Office or can be downloaded from www.environ.ie

6. Glossary

AGGREGATE

Material such as sand or small stones used, when mixed with a binder and water, to form a mortar or concrete

ANCHOR PLATE

A plate, usually of metal, fixed to the face of a wall and to which the ends of structural reinforcement, or tie bars, are bolted. Also known as a 'tie plate'

ARRIS

A sharp edge at an external angle produced by the meeting of two surfaces such as the edge of a brick

BED

The underside of a brick

BED JOINT

The horizontal mortar joint between brick courses

BRICK BOND/BONDING

The arrangement of bricks in a pattern so that each brick binds and bears upon two or more other bricks below to give strength and stability

CEMENT

A binding material mixed with aggregate and water to form a mortar or concrete. The term is usually taken to mean an artificial cement such as Ordinary Portland Cement

CLAMP

A temporary stack of unfired bricks and fuel, fired to produce finished bricks

COPING

A capping or covering to the top of a wall to prevent water entering the core of the wall

COURSE

A horizontal layer of bricks together with its bedding material

DAMP-PROOF COURSE OR DPC

An impervious layer built into a wall a little above ground level to prevent rising damp. A dpc can also be used below window sills, above lintels and beneath coping stones to prevent water penetration of the interior of the building.

DIAPER WORK

A decorative diamond patterning in face brickwork created by the use of contrasting colours of brick headers

DRESSINGS

Moulded masonry architectural features to a façade such as door and window architraves, string courses and quoins

EFFLORESCENCE

A white, powdery bloom seen on the surface of bricks caused by water in damp brickwork dissolving salts and bringing them to the surface where they are deposited as the water evaporates

FACING BRICKS

Bricks with good weather-resisting properties and a pleasing appearance, used on the external face of a wall

FAÏENCE

A type of relatively thin terracotta slab, sometimes glazed, used as a decorative cladding and usually fixed to the interior or exterior of a building in flat or moulded panels

FIRESKIN

The vitrified, protective outer layer, formed during the firing process, on the surface of bricks or terracotta units

FLAUNCHING

A sloping mortar fillet around the base of a chimney pot to hold it in place and to throw off rainwater

FROG

An indentation in one or both bed faces of a brick making it easier to handle and to bed in mortar

GAUGED BRICKWORK

Precisely-sized brickwork laid with fine mortar joints of pure lime putty and silica sand

HEADER

The exposed end face of a brick

JOINT

The mortar between two bricks

KILN

A permanent structure in which bricks are burnt or fired

MORTAR

The mixture of a binder (such as lime or cement), aggregate and water to form a substance used to bind bricks together in a masonry wall

MOULDED BRICKWORK

Bricks that are moulded before firing and built into a wall to form ornamental detail. When they have been shaped after firing they are described as cut-moulded

NOGGING

The infilling between timber studs in a partition to strengthen and stiffen them

PARAPET

The part of a wall that rises above a roof or terrace

PARGING

The application of lime mortar to the inner faces of flues to create a smooth flue and to seal any gaps

PATENT REVEAL

The vertical side of a door or window opening between the face of the wall and the frame which has received a plaster or render coating

POINTING

The application of a separate facing mortar applied onto the bedding mortar

POZZOLAN

A type of naturally-occurring volcanic ash, or any artificial substitute for it, added to a mortar to achieve a quick, strong hydraulic set

RENDER

A mixture of a binder (such as lime or cement), an aggregate and water to form a coarse plaster which is applied to the external surfaces of walls

REPOINTING

The replacement of mortar in the face joints of brickwork following either the erosion of the original mortar or its removal through raking out

RUBBER

A low-fired, high silica bearing, soft, finely grained brick, with no frog, which is can be cut or rubbed to shape (after firing) for use in gauged brickwork

RUSTICATION

In Classical architecture, the treatment of a wall surface, or part thereof, with strong texture to give emphasis and/or an impression of strength

SIZE/SIZING

A thin liquid mixture made from a natural adhesive diluted with water and applied as a sealant or filler

SNAPPED HEADERS

A brick which has been snapped in half along its stretcher length and used in face brickwork to appear as two headers

SPALLING

The gradual breaking away of small chips or flakes from the surface of individual bricks

STONEWARE

A highly vitrified ceramic made from kaolinitic clay and others minerals with a superficial appearance of natural stone

STRETCHER

The exposed long face of a brick

TERRACOTTA

Literally meaning 'burnt earth', the term is usually used to describe a more finely grained ceramic than brick or tile and is used for wall facings, chimney pots and the like

TOOTHING

Where stretchers are left protruding out of every alternative course of brickwork at the end of a wall to allow for the bonding in of future brickwork

VOUSSOIR

A wedge-shaped brick forming part of an arch

WIRECUT BRICKS

Bricks made by the extrusion of a strip of clay which is then cut by taut wires to the relevant brick size or gauge before firing

Useful contacts

The conservation officer in the local authority should be the first person to contact with queries regarding a historic building. Other useful contacts include:

Architectural Heritage Advisory Unit, Department of the Environment, Heritage and Local Government
Telephone: (01) 888 2000 Web: www.environ.ie

Building Limes Forum Ireland
Web: www.buildinglimesforumireland.com

Construction Industry Federation, Construction House, Canal Road, Dublin 6
Telephone: (01) 406 6000
Web: www.heritageregistration.ie

Heritage Council, Áras na hOidhreachta, Church Lane, Kilkenny, Co. Kilkenny
Telephone: (056) 777 0777
Web: www.heritagecouncil.ie

Irish Architectural Archive, 45 Merrion Square, Dublin 2
Telephone: (01) 663 3040
Web: www.iarc.ie

Irish Georgian Society, 74 Merrion Square, Dublin 2
Telephone: (01) 676 7053
Web: www.igs.ie

Royal Institute of the Architects of Ireland, 8 Merrion Square, Dublin 2
Telephone: (01) 676 1703
Web: www.riai.ie

Further reading

Allen, Geoffrey; Allen, Jim; Elton, Nick; Farey, Michael; Holmes, Stafford; Livesey, Paul and Radonjic, Mileva, *Hydraulic Lime Mortar for Stone, Brick and Block Masonry,* Shaftsbury: Donhead Publishing Ltd (2003)

Ashurst, John & Nicola, *Practical Building Conservation, Volume 2: Brick Terracotta & Earth,* Hampshire: Gower Technical Press (1988)

Department of the Environment, Heritage and Local Government, *Architectural Heritage Protection - guidelines for planning authorities,* Dublin: Stationery Office (2004)

Holmes, Stafford and Wingate, Michael, *Building With Lime,* Rugby: Intermediate Technology Publications (1995, revised 2002)

Keohane, Frank (ed), *Period Houses A Conservation Guidance Manual,* Dublin: Dublin Civic Trust (2001)

Lynch, Gerard, *Brickwork: History, Technology and Practice,* Shaftsbury: Donhead Publishing, Volumes 1-2 (1994)

Lynch, Gerard, 'The Colour Washing and Pencilling of Historic English Brickwork', *Journal of Architectural Conservation* Volume 12 No.6, pp 63-80

Lynch, Gerard, *Gauged Brickwork A Technical Handbook*, 2nd edition, Shaftsbury: Donhead Publishing Ltd (2007)

Lynch, Gerard, *The History of Gauged Brickwork, Conservation, Repair and Modern Application,* Oxford: Elsevier Ltd (2007)

Pavía, Sara and Bolton, Jason, *Stone, Brick and Mortar*, Bray: Wordwell Ltd (2000)

Rynne, Colin, *Industrial Ireland 1750-1930 – an archaeology,* Cork: The Collins Press (2006)

Duncannon Fort, Co. Wexford was partly repaired and rebuilt in Flemish bond brickwork during the eighteenth century